ATLAS
OF
LOST
PARADISES

Originally published as *Atlas des Paradis Perdus* by Flammarion,
Paris © 2017
Translated from the French by Rebecca DeWald

Library of Congress Control Number: 2023941031

Edited by Ian Robertson
Type set in Ethos Expanded/DTLParadoxST

ISBN: 978-0-7643-6725-0
Printed in China

Published by Schiffer Publishing, Ltd.
4880 Lower Valley Road
Atglen, PA 19310
Phone: (610) 593-1777; Fax: (610) 593-2002
Email: Info@schifferbooks.com
Web: www.schifferbooks.com

For our complete selection of fine books on this and related
subjects, please visit our website at www.schifferbooks.com. You
may also write for a free catalog.

Schiffer Publishing's titles are available at special discounts
for bulk purchases for sales promotions or premiums. Special
editions, including personalized covers, corporate imprints, and
excerpts, can be created in large quantities for special needs. For
more information, contact the publisher.

We are always looking for people to write books on new and
related subjects. If you have an idea for a book, please contact us at
proposals@schifferbooks.com.

GILLES LAPOUGE

ILLUSTRATIONS BY KARIN DOERING-FROGER

ATLAS
OF
LOST
PARADISES

CONTENTS

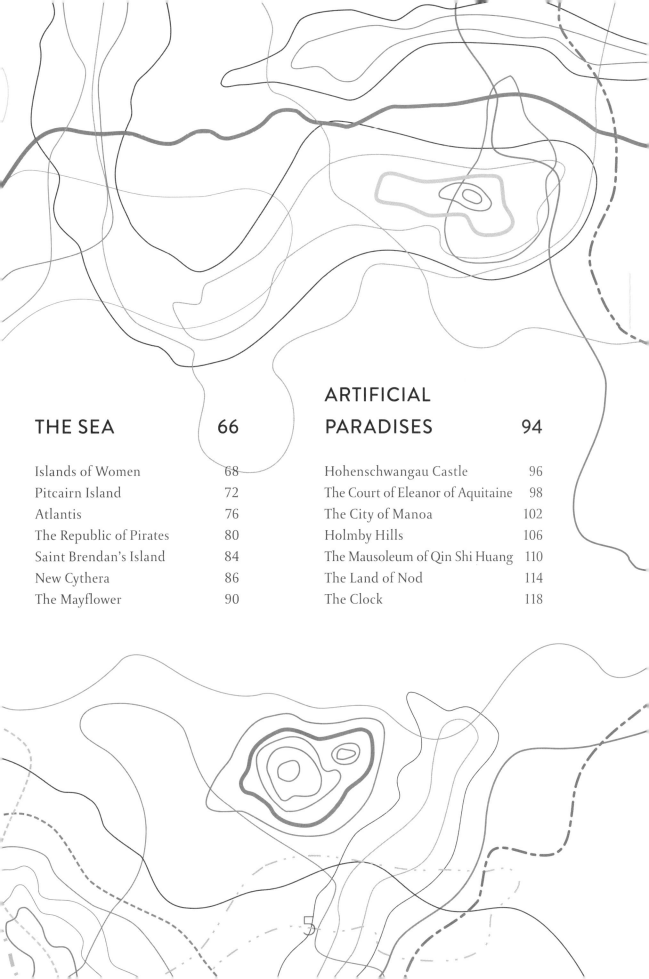

THE SEA   66

ARTIFICIAL PARADISES   94

Sancho, my friend, know that I was born, by the will of heaven, in this our iron age, to revive the one of gold, or the Golden Age, as it is called.
—Cervantes, *Don Quixote* (translated by Edith Grossman)

Paradise got off to a bad start. The one that the Bible had laid out was forced to close its gates soon after opening them, because its first two occupants, Adam and Eve, were not on their best behavior. Yet, it was still pretty successful, as Moses saw with his own eyes. It was at the meeting place of four rivers: the Pishon, which originated in the land of gold; the Gihon, which encircled the mysterious land of Kush; the Tigris; and the Euphrates. It was home to docile animals, flowers, fruit, leaves, and branches.

A little later we received good news. A second promised land—a paradise reloaded—was going to open its gates, and it would welcome people after they had breathed their last breath, provided that they had not committed too great a sin in their lifetime.

But people had become suspicious. They did not buy into the idea of having to wait until after their death to find eternal bliss. They wanted to experience happiness right away. Of course there was a whole gamut of original paradises to which people wanted to retreat: the Valhalla of the Germans, the Elysian Plains of the Greeks, the "Green Pastures" of Christians, the houris of Muslims, the nirvanas of Indian religions, and plenty of other kinds of Eden. But people never found any of them. So they decided to take charge of their own paradises and build delightful places of earthly delights, made by human hands and in such a way that they were open for the taking during one's lifetime.

Have humans been more successful in this than gods and heroes? In any case, the following great minds were ahead of their game and truly went above and beyond: Hippodamus of Miletus, Aristotle, Plato, Tommaso Campanella, Thomas More, Charles Fourier, Raymond Williams, and Étienne Cabet imagined impeccable cities clean and fair, laid out on a grid, and although they did not abolish the horror of death, they at least made it bearable. They created cities made of glass and steel, with wine bars and places that serve generous meals, the Abbey of Thelema, islands without sin or sorrow, communities governed by love and nudity, friendly neighborhoods, bird gardens and castles in the sky, beehives and chess games, merry-go-rounds and children's characters, phalansteries and homes following the motto "Do as you please," fêtes galantes, and Club Med—and for some demanding personalities even darkened rooms where certain ladies crack their whips . . . Thus dozens of types of paradise, perhaps even thousands, have been collected in books and warehouses, and the people felt reassured.

They told themselves, "It must be the devil's work or God's will if none of these gardens were to make us happy!"

The poets, for their part, would also stick their oar into the philosophers' paradises. They added splashes of colors, skies, love, and freedom to the world, and a little chaos as well, thank goodness, while engineers created scaled-down models of paradise inside clocks. Gravediggers, especially in the Chinese context, would combine the finite with eternity. An Irish saint boarded a floating island, and Cyrano de Bergerac planted his little piece of paradise on the moon. In Aquitaine, the court of Eleanor arranged lusty paradises—be they convents, brothels, or prisons. Enlightenment and nineteenth-century architects built cities of obligatory happiness—that is to say, horrors—while Ludwig II of Bavaria, the unhappy king, erected one dream castle after another. In the French theater, "paradise" refers to the top circle of the auditorium, above the boxes and balconies. In the UK this is also called "in the gods." And children also have something to say about the matter. I remember visiting paradise every summer when the Pinder or the Amar circus was in town in Digne. That was before the war. The day before, we—my friends and I—would go to the Place du Tampinet, because there is nothing more educational than witnessing the construction of a paradise. Half-naked men, like in the Garden of Earthly Delights before the Fall, armed with gigantic clubs like in the *Iliad*, rammed large stakes into the ground and tightened cables. They eventually pitched bright canvas tents under the open sky that would provide our small town with the privileges of eternity.

In the evening we would enter to see the reverse of reality. Unreal lights blinded us, enchanted us. The night was silken. Our town's irregular street layout was replaced with circles, spheres, sparkling balls, and dizziness, resembling the unfading geometries of the cosmos. People descended from the sky and would tumble into the ring. We learned that in the logic of paradise, the laws of gravity, which our teachers had drummed into our heads, were suspended, and young girls would spin around and around, topsy-turvy, near the sun and into the night.

Here wild animals were tame. They looked like creatures in fables. The lions' roar was more like a pleasant purr. They liked circles as well, it seemed. As soon as they noticed a hoop on fire, they would jump right through it without even burning themselves. Horses lighter than soap bubbles had fun climbing up on stools. We had entered the times of myths in which beasts had language. This happiness whetted our appetites for more.

The next day we would return to the Place du Tampinet, though there was barely a trace left of this paradise—just a few horse droppings, a little sawdust, and the memory of the gold and silver dancers—and we would tell ourselves that sometimes eternity can't last forever. We were tempted to drop out of school and hit the road, following in the footsteps of the circus, but we knew too well that its trailers, even if it looked like they were sticking to the highways, would travel through unknown, isolated places and that they would pitch their big tent and set up their ring and their trapezes in the evening in places where time has stood still.

Those days after the circus had left town were very sad indeed. But all this has been foretold: the Bible and the Koran, the church fathers, alchemists, schismatics and Gnostics, arch heretics and apostates, as well as Talmudists: they all had sensed their sudden and chaotic departure. Sacred texts agree on the point that paradises' destinies are not always full of glory. The Bible itself even made sure to tell us that paradise has a very sad annex: the Land of Nod, east of Eden.

We recall that the first man and the first woman had two children, Abel and Cain. The younger one, Abel, is the nice one. And his brother Cain killed him. The Lord thus cursed Cain. He drove him away and condemned him to wander the stony Land of Nod, full of horrible shrubs, sweat, and dried blood.

With Abel murdered and Cain banished to the east of Eden, Adam and Eve's legacy looked gloomy, but as Eve and her husband got older, she had another child, Seth, at the age of 120. Meanwhile, Cain continued to trudge along, east of Eden. He eventually met a woman there, Awan, who was most probably his sister, since, according to the Bible, the earth at this point did not have any other lineages. Should they commit incest? Cain and Awan discussed their options and agreed: "What does it matter?"

They had a child and called it Irad (or maybe Enoch; these stories are old and sometimes not entirely clear). What is more certain is that this child of Cain's would in turn have a child so that a new human race starts there, in the deserts of Nod—very close, yet far away, from paradise.

You see, Adam and Eve's impatience had two consequences, both equally disastrous. Of their first two children, one is killed and the other is condemned to drag his feet around a kind of reverse paradise, east of Eden, where he is forced, after committing murder, to also commit incest. These misfortunes shine a light on the human condition: most paradises turn sour, whether they are paradises imagined by higher powers or those that humankind has tried to tinker with.

There are only few success stories. Yet, failing to build paradises endowed with an eternal life expectancy, civilizations have sometimes succeeded in manufacturing small plots of Eden, a Mount Olympus in miniature, capable of pinching a few days or centuries from our endless melancholy. Gardens are one of those miracles. This is not surprising: in one of the oldest languages in the world, the Iranian language Avestan, the word *pairi-daêza* refers to a "royal or noble walled compound." In Persian, *pardêz* signifies "enclosure," and in Latin, *paradisus* has the same meaning. For the Greeks, the *parádeisos* was a "walled garden" in which wild animals were kept.

Deep down we know too well that the Garden of Eden will not reopen its gates, but we are always on the lookout for its mirror image, its fleeting precursor, in our monastic gardens; in the palm gardens and springs of Mesopotamia, Persia, or Granada; in the well-groomed parks of Versailles or Vaux-le-Vicomte; in the geometric sands of Japanese gardens; and in the exposed gardens of Scotland, as well as in the small allotments in ex-working-class cities. In summer I sometimes sneak into a tiny Garden of Eden, under the arbors of Mediterranean grapevines. There, not far from the magnificent sea, in the sun and the shade, is where the lights of wonder glisten.

Gilles Lapouge

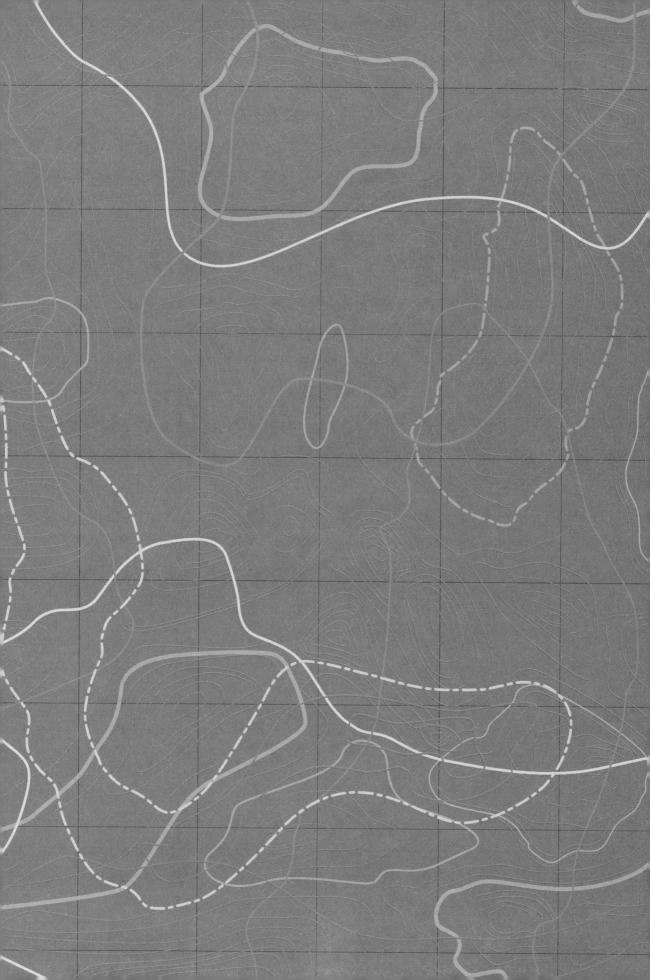

GARDENS

PERSIAN GARDENS

An Enclave of Tranquility and Eternity

A garden is a paradise. At least it presents itself as such, especially when it is Persian. The old word *pairidaēza* that appears in the Avesta, the primary collection of sacred texts of ancient Persia, which gave rise to the Greek *parádeisos* and the Latin *paradisus*, designates a space enclosed by a wall. To this place, protected from sun and sand, the gardeners of Persia would add flowers, springs, and streams. Some wild beasts and kind women would wander under the trees because sovereigns enjoyed the hunt, shade, and places conducive to the languor of love. Persia is the mother of all our gardens. The story goes that in 501 BCE, Spartan general Lysander came to the aid of the king of Persia, Cyrus the Younger, who was at war with his brother Artaxerxes II. Lysander arrived in Sardis. Cyrus received him in a vast park. The trees there were large, the soil healthy and of fine tilth, the scents of the flowers sweet, and the springs babbled. The Greek was dazzled. He expressed his admiration for the man who created this *pairidaēza*, and Cyrus swelled with pride: he had designed the paths and planted trees himself. Lysander gazed at the king, upon his "sparkling ornaments, his golds and his jewels, his purple." He exclaimed in joy: "People are right to call you lucky, Cyrus, because within you, happiness meets virtue."

The Persian garden would go on to conquer the world. It fascinated Islamic civilizations. It represents the Garden of Eden celebrated in the Koran, "for the righteous are Gardens in nearness to their Lord . . . ; therein is their eternal home." With Arab warriors, gardens would cross the Mediterranean, and the masterpieces of Al-Andalus, Madinat al-Zahra, Granada (the Alhambra), Zaragoza, etc. were created.

Such is the genius of the pairidaēza: born from the desert and imagined in sand, it can be adapted to the seasons, to people's desires, as well as to the events of history.

14

Saruhanli

Lake Marmara

Turgutlu

Sardis

Ovacık National Park

Ödemiş

Nazilli

Aydin

In India, King Babur, who descended from Timur and founded the powerful Mughal dynasty (1526–1858), was a garden architect. He built his first *pairidaēza* in Agra because he was in great need of fresh water among all this sun. He respected the Persian layout: the division of the space into four parts,

Airy pavilions, marquees, or arbors promote the warriors' relaxation and the exquisite pleasures of love.

modeled on the rules of the Charbagh. The Taj Mahal garden, commissioned by Shah Jahan (1628–1658), is the most beautiful of all Persian gardens.

Such is the genius of the *pairidaēza*: born from the desert and imagined in sand, it can be adapted to the seasons, to people's desires, as well as to the events of history. It dies in one place and is reborn elsewhere. From death to resurrections, it endures civilizations. It survived the falls of empires, and the glory and decline of dynasties. It transformed. It resisted revolutions, wars. Yet, it is also adapted to happy times. As different as it may be from the *pairidaēza*, the French garden, with its elegance, its lines of perspective, and reflections in its water features, respects the geometric inspiration of the Persian garden, although the calculations of André Le Nôtre's assistants may have been more precise than those of Cyrus. The gardens of Versailles follow a chosen geometry. Those of Old Persia celebrated a natural layout.

Is it possible to detect, if not a common plan for all Persian gardens, at least a shared inspiration? They all are enclosed by mortarless stone walls, which is an essential feature. It separates the garden, the "paradise," from the agitated turmoil of history. It creates a mysterious barricade around the beautiful garden. It turns the garden into an enclave of tranquility and near eternity in which the whirlwinds, sorrows, and frenzies of time come to a standstill. Its gardeners favor the square, occasionally replaced by a rectangle, and divide the space into four sections, separated by streams or marked paths that represent the four rivers of paradise. The source flows from the center.

"The Lord God planted a garden eastward in Eden," says the Bible, "and there He put the man whom He had formed. And out of the ground the Lord God made every tree grow that is pleasant to the sight and good for food. The tree of life was also in the midst of the garden, and the tree of the knowledge of good and evil. Now a river went out of Eden to water the garden, and from there it parted and became four riverheads."

The orchard of the Persian garden features palm trees, cypresses, plantain trees, and laurels with dark foliage, underneath which fruit and ornamental trees are planted. On the ground, in contrast with the strict arrangement of the trees, there are dazzling garlands of flowers, roses, jasmine, narcissi, marjoram, and lilies. Airy pavilions, marquees, or arbors promote the warriors' relaxation and the exquisite pleasures of love, and gazebos let visitors admire the orchards from an elevated position. A child of the desert, and invented by it, the Persian garden features multiple springs and irrigation channels commonly hidden underground.

Over time the Persian garden also ran its course. The plantain trees dropped their leaves, and the cypresses dried out. The fragile buildings made of motley wood collapsed. One fine day the babbling of the springs would be over, and the birds, these wondrous birds, would sing no more. All that remains of the gardens of Cyrus in Sardis or Pasargadae is their absence. The masterpieces of King Babur have gone with the wind. It is impossible to tell now on which terraces the Hanging Gardens of Babylon flourished, which were one of the Seven Wonders of the Ancient World and had allegedly been designed for the pleasure of a certain Queen Semiramis.

Yet, a garden never fully dies. It pretends to die. It has one advantage over every other kind of paradise: it ends, and yet it never truly ends. Less sumptuous and less eternal than those of the Bible, of Christ or the Koran, less pretentious than marbles and steles, it dies back only to be reborn. The garden is both ephemeral and perpetual, and there are still, at any given point, thousands of gardens, thousands of paradises in working order. The most humble of these, the monastic garden, with its medicinal plants, the burbling stream, and its tufts of thyme, is a tiny and indestructible Eden.

MEDIEVAL GARDENS

The Brethren of the Free Spirit

EUROPE • 48°75′ N, 07°95′ E

O miserable and very sad life!
We suffer from warfare, death and famine;
Cold and heat, day and night, sap our strength;
Fleas, scab-mites and so much other vermin
Make war upon us. In short, have mercy, Lord,
upon our wicked persons, whose life is very short.
—JEAN MESCHINOT (quoted in Johan Huizinga)

The Middle Ages got off to a bad start. It had to deal with the chaotic wreckage left behind by the Roman Empire. The ancient order was in tatters. Rainy and scorched lands, trash, epidemics and their stench, and cemeteries and mass graves heralded the new times. The chants of the destitute are like the howling of wild beasts. "Mothers," wrote Bishop Hydatius, "feasted upon the bodies of their own children whom they had killed and cooked with their own hands" (translated by R. W. Burgess). The clerics sound just like twenty-first-century philosophers prophesying the downfall of Western civilization: "So tell me, noble youth," as it says in the Carmina Burana (circa 1225), what you have in mind! | Is it silver now the prize, in your words enshrined, | or a precious jewel that dazzled eyes may blind? | If I can I'll give to you whate'er you seek to find" (translated by A. S. Kline). The poet Guiot de Provins wrote, "The men of the past were great, beautiful. Nowadays, they are children and dwarves."

But the Middle Ages cannot be reduced to simply deploring the olden days. Hungry for a golden age, they were eager to reenter the beautiful garden. As soon as things got a little better—from the twelfth century onward—sects multiplied. They provided recipes that would allow people to escape the darkness, blood, sin, and evil. The idea was to go back in time and let history unfold backward. This way, the world would be purged of its history and blessed again, indifferent to the devil's little schemes.

Rather than wasting away in a dungeon of sin, lovers in the golden age chose to reopen the gates to paradise from which the first couple was evicted because of their curiosity about science and sex. Many had "fallen from grace." In the Rhineland and the Netherlands, then in France and Paris itself, an amorphous grouping of sects formed around the Brethren of the Free Spirit, the Amalricians, the Adamites, the turlupins, a couple of Beguines and Beghards, without there being any discernible differences between these sects.

18

Most of them recommended poverty to purify the soul and cleanse it of all its sins. Unfortunately, some disciples concluded that therefore "property is theft." They attacked the rich, persecuted them, took up residence in the houses of others, destroyed their land, and even killed them.

The Adamites tackled one of the most unfortunate consequences of the original sin: sexual mores. Their proposal was attractive indeed: those wanting to regain the innocence of the Garden of Eden, they suggested, must imitate Adam before the Fall. For the Brethren of the Free Spirit, those who fornicate persistently were "discerning in spirit." They even renamed the sexual act and called it instead the "delights of Paradise," and that should do the trick: the Garden of Wonders would reopen its

Heaven is now on Earth, sin does not exist, and hell is sheer humbug.

gates. Heaven is now on Earth, sin does not exist, and hell is sheer humbug.

The *Mirror of Simple Souls* by Marguerite Porète provides some details: "The soul that has been annihilated in God's love can surrender to Nature. It can consume all it desires, without remorse. If you want Paradise, listen to your desires." Marguerite saw no difference between carnal love and charity. In 1310 she was burned at the stake in Paris, with the approval of Philip the Fair.

Another group, the turlupins, was impatient. They wanted paradise and they wanted it now. They were frank about it. They thought that humanity was generous and that the earth was a place of happiness. So they made love to one another as often as they wanted. The tragedy of the Fall, they thought, was a fable. Ignore the original sin and you will enter a universe without evil! To abolish the misdeeds of history, they had a trick up their sleeves: you had to take your clothes off. So they threw their clothes down the mills. Hundreds of thousands, even millions of men and women at the heart of Europe were naked and did not hesitate to make love in public like bonobos. One of the leaders of this sect exuded great authority. That was because he claimed to have been lucky enough to learn just how Adam made love to Eve, and out of the goodness of his heart, he wanted to communicate this secret to his brothers and sisters.

Haguenau

La Wantzenau •

Rhine

Rastatt

Rhine

Drusenheim

fendorf
Forest
Nature
eserve

Lichtenau

Waldhägenich

Rheinau

INVEREWE GARDENS

Fashioning a Garden of Eden out of Nothing

———

EUROPE • 57°46' N, 05°36' W

In 1862, Lady Mackenzie of Gairloch made over property to her son, Lord Osgood Mackenzie. It was a large gift: 2,100 acres (850 hectares). Unfortunately, the area was not just in Scotland but in Inverewe, near Loch Ewe, to be precise, on the fifty-eighth parallel north, so fairly close to the Arctic Circle. Clouds and spindrift characterize Inverewe, with plenty of storms and overcast skies. In terms of vegetation, this stretch of land was characterized by its salty soil covered in pebbles, sad grasslands, and one single tree, a willow, which looked rather depressing as well. The Scots were well versed in the Bible. So the young lord probably understood that his mother had gifted him a piece of land situated "east of Eden." He found himself the master of a humid and stormy plot, a version of the Land of Nod in which the unfortunate Cain had been wandering for some eternity now. So Osgood Mackenzie rolled up his Scottish sleeves and got to work.

He bought soil from Ireland and dumped it on to this barren land. He cordoned off a plot of about 50 acres (20 hectares) by erecting walls around it, as if he remembered that the word *parádeisos*, which means "paradise" in Greek, first referred to a space enclosed by walls. A miniclimate developed there, favored by the Gulf Stream, which

flows not far from here and comes all the way from the Caribbean. Then Lord Mackenzie planted all kinds of trees. From time to time, the sky would change its mood and produce a storm reminiscent of the end or the beginning of the world, after which Lord Osgood, brave like someone in Jean de La Fontaine's *Fables*, would just get back to work. He would dig in his spade and keep planting. Whenever possible, he would buy trees from tropical and distant countries, such as New Zealand, Australia, or South Africa. He turned the scarce moorland of Inverewe into a riot of color. Here you can admire Scots pine with its red bark, eucalyptus trees from Tasmania, Chilean nasturtiums, and rhododendrons from around the world (including Tibet, China, and Tasmania, and some from Chile that would wilt if it got too cold). You can look at birch and rowan trees, a huge cherry tree from Japan, giant rhubarb from Brazil, blue poppies, Chilean lantern trees, erythronium from California, myrtle, and countless varieties of lichen, one of which looks like silver. But Osgood Mackenzie and his successors were never satisfied. They replanted the whole world in this sea mist: the Inverewe Peninsula would eventually reflect the five continents.

The Scottish lord and his successors subjected the land to their laws. They corrected its geography.

22

They transported the equator within reach of the North Pole. This makes one think of the nineteenth-century French utopian François-Marie-Charles Fourier, who proposed to redistribute the cities on the map of the world by moving South America a little farther north, and suggesting that the pleasant climate of Andalusia could extend to the North Pole. The Scottish lord did better than the French philosopher because he put words into action. He made his daydreams tangible and real. He manipulated space and geography. And he did even more than that: he rearranged time and history as he pleased. Inverewe Gardens feature nine Wollemi conifers, an Australian tree that has all but disappeared nowadays but has long existed in our imagination, since herbivore di-

The Inverewe peninsula would eventually reflect the five continents.

nosaurs used to graze on its foliage.

French politician and novelist Érik Orsenna, who knows his flowers, visited Inverewe. He muses that the Mackenzie dynasty wanted to "repatriate the treasure before the flood." The "treasure" he refers to is the Commonwealth, the empire on which the sun never sets, and the "flood" is the hiccup of history that would tear apart Queen Victoria's dominion after World War II. There, toward the North Pole, the British Empire would continue to exist in the form of flowers, bark, lichen, and rhododendrons pinched from the gardens of officers in the Indian army or from elegant ladies in Kenya.

I, for my part, see in the adventure of Inverewe Gardens the epilogue of the tribulations of our forefathers after they had committed the sin of nudity, causing both the closure of the beautiful Garden of Eden and the misfortune of their children: the elder, Abel, finding his death, and the younger, Cain, imprisoned in the infinite steppe that extends east of Eden.

The miracle of Inverewe creeps into the story of the first adventure of humankind. Lord Osgood Mackenzie, although he did not kill his brother, inherited a piece of land as barren as the Land of Nod. But instead of resigning himself to his fate, as Cain did, by pacing both throughout eternity and the void, he turned his misty patch of land into a tropical dream, a Garden of Eden. If my hypothesis is sound, it is also reassuring, since it suggests that paradises can sometimes be resurrected, even after they have been cursed.

Loch
Thurnaig

Inverewe
●

● Londubh

MOUNT PENGLAI

In Pursuit of the Immortals

ASIA • 37°48' N, 120°45' E

« Paradise exists in heaven, and Suzhou and Hangzhou on earth.»

The Chinese garden has something in common with Persian, Arabic, Scottish, Italian, and Luxembourgish gardens: it is modeled on paradise, which invites us to take a detour to explore what the Chinese paradise looks like. It sits atop a distant mountain, Mount Penglai, on an island east of the Bohai Sea. On a clear day, a few lucky ones have been able to see the palaces in which the Immortals reside. These palaces are made of gold and jade, some say even of platinum. Its birds are of a pure white. Trees here commonly sprout jewelry, but the Tree of Wonders gifts immortality to those who eat its fruits. We have little information about these Immortals because they are too fast. They spin like the wind. Some claim that the only chance to perceive Penglai is to see its mirage, upside down, when the sea is still. Emperor Qin Shi Huang (259–210 BCE), an anxious man who did not like death, sent one of his alchemists to Penglai, probably to ask the Immortals for tips, but the al-

chemist returned empty-handed. Qin Shi Huang made further attempts, but all the boats disappeared at sea. So he had the mountain painted red.

The Chinese garden reflects the lessons taught by paradise: mountains, trees, water, and islands play a major role in it. Bamboo, pine trees, peonies, and lotuses represent the forest. And there is water everywhere. This water is cleansing, sometimes pooled in ponds where carp swim, or lively, fresh and flowing, in brooks, torrents, and waterfalls. Complex rock formations stand in for the mountain. They come in irregular shapes, feature plenty of cracks or holes, and are full of empty spaces. Sculptures represent animals: the turtle, the dragon, the phoenix.

The Chinese gardener, unlike his colleague from Versailles or Villandry, is not subjected to strict geometries. Symmetry is not its strong point, and its layout is vague and shifty. It avoids straight lines that could attract demons. The Chinese do not claim to dominate nature. They choose to depict harmony within things.

They compose nature in a sublimated way, simultaneously real and, mysteriously, at the edge of reality. The Chinese garden is a miniature cosmos. "A world in a grain of rice," as they say—a pretty saying, a little childish maybe, though it summarizes the task of the gardener: to fit the whole universe into a small space and make manifest the magic of nature.

Light and plays of light are among the key ingredients of the Chinese garden: the changing seasons, the return of color with each bloom, encroaching shadows, and the evening; these all represent the change of things and their return.

Architecture is not absent from these spaces either. The garden is structured by buildings of various shapes and serving different purposes: marquees and pavilions, pagodas, and arches, as well as bridges and arbors. While elements taken from nature (yin) are free from any constraint, the built-up sec-

tions, on the contrary (yang), are arranged along an axis. Open spaces are carefully plotted here and there that let the visitor contemplate the beauty and secrets of nature within interlacing paths, ponds, walls, and groves. Light and plays of light are among the key ingredients of the Chinese garden: the changing seasons, the return of color with each bloom, encroaching shadows, and the evening; these all represent the change of things and their return.

China has a long history. The garden evolves, transforms, and is enriched over the centuries. Scholars say that this art—as well respected as calligraphy—reached its peak during the Ming dynasty, which corresponds to the late Middle Ages and the Early Modern period in the West. In the eighteenth century, missionaries made the art of the Western garden known in China—and the Chinese succumbed to its seduction. The Chinese garden subsequently fell into decline and died out. Like most paradises, this one would disappear, but it would do so in silence, far from the noise and fury that usually accompanies the end of happiness.

Tanglang Island

Daheishan
Island

Penglai

Longkou
Port

Luoshan
National
Forest Park

Zhaoyuan

Yellow
Sea

aozi
ay

Weihai •

• Yantai

Kunyushan
National
Forest Park

nzhen

DIGNE-LES-BAINS

A Childhood Paradise

———— ◆ ————

For a long time I lived in paradise. And I didn't even realize. My parents hadn't told me. They were not aware of it. It must be said that any paradise that had come to set up shop in the sleepy little town of Digne would have not been a very clever paradise at all. Or it must have been a misplaced par-

From time to time, and indeed every single morning, I was banished from paradise because I had to take my satchel, walk across our small town, and spend the day at school.

adise, maybe even a paradise driven out of paradise itself for bad behavior.

Ours did its best to live up to its name: at the center of our rectangular garden reigned a very large magnolia tree that had been planted by my grandfather, who was from another century and still wore vests, black ankle boots, and a pince-nez. The magnolia was the tree of good and evil and repre-

sented the knowledge of oneself. It was surrounded by a hedge of rather sickly-looking spindle trees arranged in a circle.

Four paths led from this round of sickly trees toward the four cardinal points. When Priest Olivier, who taught us our catechism, got to the Bible, I immediately understood that these four paths represented the four rivers that once irrigated Eden: Tigris, Euphrates, Gihon, and Pishon. These paths split our garden into four equal sections modeled on the Persian *pairidaēza*.

Like all paradises, ours was surrounded by a wall that sheltered us from the noise of trucks, the mischief of loiterers, and, in general, the discomfort of our time. In doing so, it also protected us from death. It carved out a plot of eternity where we were at ease. This kind of feature was not at all unusual. Several gardens in our neighborhood were designed according to the same pattern, just like medieval cloister gardens: a central tree, a circle of spindle trees, a wall, a large square garden, and four paths that represented the rivers Euphrates, Tigris, etc. I concluded, with a little pride, that we were among the lucky ones:

Mercantour
National Park

● Digne-les-bains

Saint-André-
les-Alpes
●

anosque

Sainte-Croix-
du-Verdon ●

Verdon Regional
Nature Park

Brignoles ●

Our neighborhood, although it was called La Sèbe ("onion" in Provençal), was a haven of paradises.

From time to time, and indeed every single morning, I was banished from paradise be-

My daily to the Land of Nod, east of Eden, ensured that my paradise had a life expectancy rarely granted to ordinary paradises.

cause I had to take my satchel, walk across our small town, and spend the day at school. There a nun reigned with an iron fist. Her name was Ernestine, but we called her Titine. The cheekiest among us called her "Titine Aubergine": Titine Eggplant. She was a harsh mistress and made us realize that we

were now east of Eden, in the Land of Nod, where poor Cain continued to wander since he had killed his brother.

Each night, the exile ended and I returned home, to the garden, and I thought to myself that my paradise was beautifully laid out.

Its inventors had thought it through. They understood that an eternal paradise would not work. Its delights must stop from time to time, or else they would lose their appeal and even become irritating. My daily visits to the Land of Nod, east of Eden, ensured that my paradise had a life expectancy rarely granted to ordinary paradises, such as Canaan, the heaven mentioned in *The Tibetan Book of the Dead* or the Muslim Jannah, "as vast as the heavens," where those reside who fear Allah.

The magnolia tree is still there and keeps growing. It is majestic. Every summer I set up a deck chair in its shade and I think of the very dear, very beautiful, very sweet Titine Aubergine.

UTOPIAS

FONTEVRAUD ABBEY

When Paradise Turns into Hell

———————

EUROPE • 47°10' N, 00°03' E

*I am the slave of my baptism. You,
my parents, have ruined my life,
and your own. Poor child!—Hell is
powerless against pagans.*

—ARTHUR RIMBAUD (translated by Andrew Jary)

Monasteries are out of this world. They pretend to reside among us, in our countryside, but, protected by their silence, their gardens, their rules, and their walls, they are removed from secular spaces. They are not slaves to the rhythms and needs of society. Their citizens form an "order," not a "nation." They are not subjected to "laws," which are temporary constructs, but to a "rule" that, like the stars in the sky, is beyond the possibility of "adaptation" or "reformation."

The convent does not care about the wishes of the monks, their appetites, their desires, the states of their souls, or the illusions of the world outside. Whether he is a lay monk or ordained, the brother is only a cog in the wheel. Every day is the same. They each escape the ruses of time. Freed from history and the seasons, from psychology, desires, and sorrows, even rid of their names, monks become "men without qualities."

Admittedly, while paradise spares its residents the inconvenience of death, even monks pass away from time to time, but their demise is only illusory, since a Carthusian or a Trappist has already been robbed of his identity during his lifetime. He left it at the door of the monastery as if tossing out an old shoe. With this gesture he has renounced his family to become a being without a name, without predecessors or successors, without a past or a future. Saved from the traps of psychology and the illusions of history, the monk has nestled into an eternal now.

Fontevraud is the largest abbey in Europe. It works very well. It is true that its founder, Robert d'Arbrissel (eleventh century), had entrusted its direction to women because Jesus had said on the Cross, "Woman, behold thy son!" and to his disciple, "Behold thy mother!" Fontevraud was a double monastery, for monks and nuns. Robert d'Arbrissel had such respect for femininity that he slept naked among nude young girls to resist the temptations of the flesh.

This habit deprived him of the privileges of holiness, Rome having judged his asceticism odd, and even dangerous, since souls of a less firm constitution could easily succumb to the temptation.

Sometimes the monks lost their temper because they did not like women giving them orders. They rioted and ran away, but Rome would always tell them they were in the wrong, and they had to resign themselves to their situation. Over five centuries, one abbess succeeded another. They governed wisely with the help of "informer nuns," who were entrusted with the task of identifying those who "idled, chatted, or snoozed." The nuns were entitled to wine rations that were twice as generous as those of the monks.

Immune to history, Fontevraud endured more than five centuries. On the other side of its visible and invisible walls, history was in turmoil, but the abbey was not troubled by it. In the end, however, the outbreak of the French Revolution got the better of its serenity. On June 2, 1791, the last abbess left. Looters destroyed the sarcophagi, damaged the tomb effigies, and scattered the bones; ten years later, in 1804, Napoleon decided to repurpose these abandoned buildings. The emperor, never short of ideas, had an-

other flash of inspiration. He would turn Fontevraud into a prison. Paradise had become hell, which is just as well, because hell is, after all, just another form of paradise: an enclosed space, excluded from the turmoil of history, and since it is cut off from time, so are its inhabitants, who have had to exchange their names for numbers. The inmates are stripped of the advantages of this world and forced to make the same repetitive gestures every day and every second. Eventually subjected to a cold and implacable rule, they become, like anchorites and anchoresses, or Benedictines, people "without qualities."

Fontevraud teaches us a dark lesson. It posits that paradises, at least those built by human hand, are not everlasting. Credit to Napoleon for taking this analysis one step further by demonstrating that if hell is the opposite of paradise, both are made up of the same ingredients. The springs and valves that adjust their movements are approximately the same. The only difference is that one is the hearth of absolute goodness and the other of definitive evil. Unfortunately the walls separating heaven and hell are sometimes porous . . .

Tours

Loire

Loire-Anjou Touraine
Regional
Nature Park

Vienne

Châtellerault

Brenne
Regional
Nature Park

THE HOUSE OF PLEASURES

The Union of Devotion and Lust

———————

EUROPE • 49°14' N, 07°00' E

A paradise of sadness.

—PAUL CLAUDEL

Europe has no shortage of paradises. They come in all sorts of shapes and sizes. The most famous is in La Jonquera, on the border between Spain and France. On another border, in Saarbrücken, not far from the Maginot Line that France had drawn back in the day to scare off Hitler's panzer divisions, reigns another Eden, the FKK Paradise, where young women with bare breasts wander through the rooms and are joined in the evenings by excited men from France or Germany.

One may deplore that the extraordinary garden imagined by the Lord to reward deserving individuals nowadays serves as a symbol of debauchery. But that, too, has a long tradition. In 1871 in France, exhausted by the fight against the Germans and then by the assassination of the Communards, a brothel opened its doors. It was called "Le Paradis."

This union between devotion and lust is as old as the hills. It was celebrated by François Villon, who was a tough boy, then by Chateau-briand, who was a Peer of France and whose specialist subject was *The Genius of Christianity*. In his *Mémoires d'Outre-Tombe*, he wrote, "In Niort there was a house of debauchery modeled on an abbey." Until 1946 there was a famous brothel in Paris called the Abbey. Indeed, it was very close to the Saint-Sulpice Church, at 36 rue Saint-Sulpice. Since it was reserved for clergymen, its rooms were called the Sacristy or the Confessional. And since paradises easily lead to hell, one of these cells was even called Satan. It was kitted out with the right equipment: chains, crucifixes, handcuffs, and lots of costumes.

The names given to brothels in popular language confirm Chateaubriand's intuitions. By pushing the door of a "house of ill repute," one enters a "den of iniquity." In the brothel, as in the abbey, the rules of secular society are overturned or become obsolete. The "private quarters," a term that covers all brothels, exist on land that looks as if it belongs to our geography, but in fact it occupies another space.

In 1944, brothels were off-limits for American soldiers. Like convents, abbeys, and Trappist and Carthusian orders, bordellos occupied

40

Kaiserslautern

Saarbrücken

Forbach

Metz

Northern Vosges
Regional
Nature Park

Nancy

Strasbourg

Ballon des Vosges
Regional
Nature Park

Épinal

wastelands and even no-man's land. The brothel is not quite of this world. It is a "little corner of paradise." The laws that the nation-state imposes on us have no validity in its half light. The red light that signals a house of ill repute marks entry onto a delicious, dangerous, and perhaps diabolical terrain.

A brothel in French is also called a *maison close*: an enclosed house, a sealed system, making up its own rules and drawing on

In the brothel, as in the abbey, the rules of secular society are overturned or become obsolete.

its own powers, without communication with the "big wide world." Prayers, flagellations, pleasures, or ecstasies: everything the brothel generates is produced on-site and by hand. The brothel, like the monastery, is self-sufficient. Its clients don't have identities. No one knows where the punters come from. They enjoy a short stint in ecstasy before disappearing and returning to the profanity of the city. Some up-market bordellos provide their clients with alternative

identities and costumes of their dreams. A plumber becomes a retired general. A surveyor turns into a notary, a gardener is made up as a bishop and, to top it off, he gets to screw a nun.

Strict convents such as the Trappists or the Carthusians do not proceed any differently. At the entrance to the monastery, at the wall, the novice is given a new name and an unusual habit. He becomes mute and learns that he no longer has a family. All he has left to do is to live and die.

The ladies who inhabit the brothel are subjected to similar rites. They are given new names, they put on clothes they would not wear in the streets, they get naked at the drop of a hat, which sets them apart from society, and when they engage in carnal knowledge, they act without desire or passion, without attachment, memory, or enjoyment.

The difference between them and the Trappist is that the latter has to put on his new identity for his entire life, while in the house of pleasure, the plumber is a bishop only to get a little jiggy. He then hurries back to his secular home because, if he is late, his wife will scorn him that the roast is now overcooked.

At this point there is a noticeable difference between the convent and the brothel: in the monastery, time extends to infinity. A man or woman commits for a lifetime, and even for some eternity. Monastic life is slow, almost immobile. In the paradise of bodies, the opposite is the case: the rhythms are accelerated. For example, let us imagine the highlight of many lives as it would play out in a brothel: a wedding, but as a sped-up Charlie Chaplin movie. The young man and woman meet, fancy each other in the blink of an eye, flirt fervently, reduce the time of their engagement to a split second, consummate their marriage within half an hour, and get divorced again.

Apart from Chateaubriand, believers generally pass over these connections between the paradise of monks and that of prostitutes. Yet, religion itself gets straight to the point and admits the link. Muhammad went on a night journey from Mecca to Jerusalem, on the 27th of Rajab in the year II before the Hijrah, in the company of the angel Jibreel (Gabriel). During the journey he had the opportunity to perceive some beings from the "beyond." The Muslim paradise is a pleasant place. It enjoys an ideal climate, and its gardens are abundant with ferocious and docile beasts, fountains, springs, rivers, and flowers of all colors.

In this garden, men have everything they need to be happy. The food is healthful. The wine flows nonstop. And the faithful have houris at their disposal, beautiful young girls with large, velvety black eyes. They are all the same age, and all of them have shapely breasts. This paradise has managed to avoid the pitfall that commonly breaks the camel's back: the act of love. Here, carnal pleasures are not only accepted, but highly encouraged.

Yet, there is one downside: although men have everything they need to spend their eternity without getting bored, the fate of young women is less pleasant. Having to devote themselves to the contentment of faithful men, and condemned to pleasuring without experiencing any pleasure themselves, since, according to Ibn Qayyim al-Jawziyya, they are "free from an umbilical cord, childbirth, and menses, and pure of mucous, saliva, urine, and other filthy things," their paradise is somewhat of a letdown. Was the poet Arthur Rimbaud thinking about this two-tier paradise when he exclaimed, "I went through women's Hell over there" (translated by Andrew Jay)?

THE DÉSERT DE RETZ

The Sum of All Landscapes and Civilizations

Isaiah predicted that one day the desert would bloom like a narcissus. Deserts are popular with shepherds, gods, prophets, and wise men. They boast all that your heart could desire: infinity, skies and sand, pebbles, thirst and blinding light, and the beauty of the night; there is nowhere better to simultaneously give over your soul to abandon and splendor. The desert works like an "interchange" between the here and the beyond.

It has created gods and religions. Muhammad sought seclusion in the Cave of Hira, in the desert of the Jabal al-Nour mountain, where the archangel Jibreel came to see him. Muhammad is intimidated at first. Jibreel talks to him. Back in Mecca, Muhammad then proclaims the word of God.

Abraham was also a man of the desert, and the prophet Hosea is warned about his wife: "I will allure her and bring her into the wilderness and speak comfortably unto her." Later, Moses spent forty years in the desert, which seemed to him "great and terrible." Here he meets Yahweh. For his part, Christ begins his public life with a forty-day seclusion in the wilderness. The devil tries to tempt him. Fortunately Jesus does not flinch. The Désert de Retz is less grandiose than Mount Sinai or the rocky Negev Desert of Palestine. The man who created it in the eighteenth cen-

tury, Henri Racine de Monville, was less ambitious than Muhammad or Jesus. His model was Alceste, the protagonist of Molière's *The Misanthrope*, who has a foul temper and chooses the "desert" to put an end to the affectations, hypocrisies, and treacheries of court life.

"And sometimes," Alceste says, "I feel suddenly inclined to fly into a wilderness far from the approach of men" (I, 1, v. 143–144; anonymous translator).

Monsieur de Monville, in contrast, is an attractive man. Very rich and beautiful, a virtuoso horse rider and flute player, he is also capable of shooting down a pheasant with a bow and arrow. He has a passion for botany. In 1777 he places an enormous order with the royal nursery: thousands of predominantly exotic plants. On his property at Chambourcy, on the edge of the Fôret de Marly, he would create one of the most beautiful gardens of the Enlightenment era.

The huge estate is full of pavilions that Monsieur de Monville called "factories." Less grumpy than his role model Alceste, he would invite the crème de la crème of European art to his retreat: poets, musicians, dancers. He played the lute with composer Christoph Gluck, Madame du Barry, Queen Marie Antoinette, King Gustav III of Sweden, Thomas Jefferson, and the marvelous Belgian Prince of Ligne:

in short, all the VIPs of the Enlightenment visited the Désert de Retz.

We can name only a couple of his factories here. There is the Pyramid Icehouse, used to keep ice to make sorbets. A young architect who supervised the construction works prided himself on having had the idea for this fridge. Monville was seething and chased the insolent person away. Another factory, the Hermitage, was a wooden hut in which visitors could admire a hermit paid by Monville to never wash and to cut neither his nails nor his hair.

The desert featured vast landscapes, a herb garden, dingley dells, a pond, an "island of happiness," an Anglo-Chinese garden, trees of precious wood, and a sylvan theater.

Among these factories we must also mention the Tartar tent clad with toile de Jouy, the Chinese Pavilion, which was the first Chinese house in Europe, a ruined Gothic church, the temple to the god Pan, an ancient Roman altar, the Temple of Repose, the Tomb, an orangery, a dairy, a tenant small holding, and many more. Monsieur de Monville was truly a "universal man." He turned his desert into the sum of all landscapes, of all civilizations.

The most curious factory is the *colonne détruite*: the destroyed column. Measuring 82 feet tall (25 meters) and 49 feet (15 meters) in diameter, it houses apartments over six floors arranged around a central spiral staircase. The rooms are sumptuous, featuring mirrors, acanthus leaves, and mahogany furniture. This column is made to look like the ruin of a huge Roman temple that has since ceased to exist. It was built in 1781. For Monsieur de Monville, who might have been a Freemason, it symbolized the future ruin of the European order, destroyed under the blows of the French Revolution.

The Désert de Retz would indeed succumb to the upheavals of 1792. Monsieur de Monville would be saved a fate under the guillotine thanks to the fall of Robespierre. He died in 1797, bankrupted by his mistresses. Thus began the time of decline. The estate slowly fell into disrepair. It would eventually live up to its name and become a "desert" again. The rare plants and flowers wilted, and the pavilions, temples, and columns collapsed. The surrealists, who loved ruins, celebrated the defunct beauty of the Désert de Retz.

Colette, who knew all the gardens of France, called this one "my earthly paradise." And she is right. Sometimes paradises fall into ruin.

In 1965, André Malraux became a minister in General de Gaulle's government. And Désert de Retz is slowly reborn.

45

● Montmorency

Argenteuil ●

Bois de
Boulogne

● Paris

...sailles

National
Forest of
Meudon

THE BEGUINAGES

Life without Rules

Agatha, does your heart rise up and fly,
Far from the city's black and sordid sea
Towards a sea that's blue as any sky,
Blue, clear, deep, as well as virginity?
Agatha, does your heart rise up and fly?

—CHARLES BAUDELAIRE

Theologians generally advise that one must die before entering paradise, but some impatient people prefer to create small paradises on the spot, to enjoy the delights of a beautiful garden during their lifetime. Convents constitute one type of these paradises on Earth. There, in beautiful and even sumptuous houses, sheltered from the noise of the world, men or women form harmonious societies dedicated to prayer, chastity, work, and singing the heavens' praises. However, these communities have one disadvantage: they require that their members leave at the door of the convent everything that gives the human condition its appeal—wealth, lust, jealousy, pride, selfishness, and glory. Without making these sacrifices, you have no chance of achieving holiness, and the sweet delights of heaven will run through your fingers. This is why some apostates won't let themselves be enlisted in these holy squads and try instead to reconcile the happiness of eternity with that of the here and now.

In the Middle Ages, the influential women's movement of the Beguines imagined that the demands of heaven could be combined with the freedoms of secular life. The first beguinages opened their doors in the twelfth century in Liège and spread from there throughout northern Europe. The Beguines lived in small, very charming individual houses, grouped together not far from the parish church. Although pious, they were laywomen. They were free and lived under joint leadership. There was no common law and no mother superior. Each beguinage defined its own rules, or rather the absence of rules. A Beguine was a free woman, often unmarried or widowed. She had the right to make a vow; for example, a vow of chastity, to inhibit her sensuality. She could even utter the same vow as a married woman for the "benefit" of her husband (the poor guy).

Beguines prayed a lot. They would also work as aides in hospitals. They ran their own weaving workshops, which displeased weavers' guilds. Excellent handywomen, they made candles and carded wool, and the most skillful among them painted sacred paintings or copied holy texts. They were called "beggar nuns" and enjoyed dazzling success: beguinages were everywhere. In these sheltered places, women could celebrate the glory of God as they pleased while avoiding the disciplines of monastic life.

Each beguinage defined its own rules, or rather the absence of rules.

At first the Beguines recruited among the working classes, but they soon seduced sophisticated and very rich bourgeois women who moved into the small houses, delighted to be able to lead a life dedicated to God while escaping the rules of an order, the demands of a husband, and the harshness of a strict mother superior.

The church initially observed this spiritual yet secular movement with benevolence. It found the virtues practiced in or recommended by the beguinages—work, poverty, and prayer—in line with its own rules. Later, as their success grew, the bishops began to worry. They also noticed that kings and some powerful lords gave bequests and large donations to beguinages, which posed the risk of reducing their donations to monastic or secular orders. And on top of that, these women were weird. Freed from any kind of male grip, they had developed an unbridled need for freedom.

That did not sit well with the high church, which was not too keen on the idea of freedom. If these fans of absolute freedom had been men, their bad luck might have been only half as bad. But Beguines were women, and women, as we know, are one of Satan's favorite treats.

The bishops were also beginning to wonder if these people, under the guise of advocating work, poverty, prayer, and good deeds, were not inoculating the church itself with the most fetid of poisons: freedom. We all know how it works: you grant someone a fraction of freedom, and before you can say, "Jack Robinson," all institutions collapse, disorder ensues, and impiety triumphs.

Furthermore, they were fanatics. Douceline de Digne, who took the Beguines' veil in 1240, would put on a pigskin, never to take it off again. Whenever her entourage

But Beguines were women, and women, as we know, are one of Satan's favorite treats.

ripped it off her, the Beguine's own skin came off along with that of the pig. Douceline did not stop there. She would add to the pig skin a belt of thorns that caused her purulent wounds in which worms began to jiggle. She died at the age of thirty-five, though had performed miracles in her lifetime and gained beatification.

These women, hungry for freedom, were beginning to put a strain on age-old hierarchies. The Beguines rejected not only sec-

ular institutions but the Catholic Church itself. They skirted around morality. The bishops frowned upon it. In 1233 the inquisitor Konrad von Marburg cursed them. In 1310, Marguerite Porète, who recommended annihilating one's soul so as to fill it with God's love and become God oneself, was burned at the stake. Pope Clement V condemned the Beguines and declared them to be heresiarchs.

The Beguines would suffer a long and painful death. They would disappear from all over Europe except in Flanders, where they managed to become tolerated by the church. The memory of their noble adventure, however, has not faded. Here and there would be brief resurrections, such as in Germany and France. In 1951, Flemish Belgian novelist Françoise Mallet-Joris, who would later become a member of the Académie Goncourt, wrote a beautiful novel, *Le rempart des Béguines* (*The Illusionist*, translated by Herma Briffault), set in a beguinage, which tells of a passionate love between two women.

CECÍLIA COLONY

An Anarchist Dream

SOUTH AMERICA • 25°25′, 50°00′ W

I must add, besides, that my system is not yet complete. . . . I am perplexed by my own data, and my conclusion is a direct contradiction of the original idea with which I start. Starting from unlimited freedom, I arrive at unlimited despotism.

—Fiodor Dostoïevski (translated by Constance Garnett)

In 1897, Pedro de Alcântara João Carlos Leopoldo Salvador Bibiano Francisco Xavier de Paula Leocádio Miguel Gabriel Rafael Gonzaga de Bragança e Habsburgo traveled to Italy. There he met a vet who went by the name Giovanni Rossi. The first offered the latter a plot of land in Brazil. This did not surprise Giovanni Rossi, since the aforesaid Pedro was in fact Emperor Dom Pedro II, who had ruled Brazil for fifty years. And since Rossi was an anarchist, he accepted the gift and enlisted some of his friends: ten men and a woman by the name of Olympia. The group settled in Brazil, in the state of Paraná, where they founded an anarchist colony. They wanted to prove that human-

ity was capable of creating small paradises: peaceful, happy communities without oppression or hierarchy, living in freedom and respect—once the poisons of bourgeois society had been eradicated. At that time, European anarchists were mainly busy blowing up public buildings and killing people. Rossi would demonstrate that anarchy was just as suitable for fomenting happiness and forging paradises on Earth.

> *Rossi would demonstrate that anarchy was just as suitable for fomenting happiness and forging paradises on Earth.*

They got off to a good start. People at Cecília worked hard and ate little. The colony grew. It would house up to 150 people, but the famous Italian anarchist Errico Malatesta was not pleased. He did not like the Cecília Colony one bit.

He found Giovanni Rossi to be a "traitor" and a "deserter."

On top of that, the colony was running out of steam. Because of the lack of money, food was bought on credit. The colony loaned some of its members to the Brazilian government to build roads. Rossi suddenly believed that "anarchy has prostituted itself intellectually" and has been replaced by "dictatorship and parliamentarism." So instead of electing a leader, Cecília Colony would therefore be governed through referendums. And that didn't work. Rossi planned to return to his profession as a vet, and Cecília was set to vanish.

In June 1891, seven families fled and stole cattle. There was a brief moment of calm with the arrival of some Italian peasants, but these farmers were "tightwads" and wary of everyone else. Cecília had become one long argument. Rossi had one last card up his sleeve. He would allow free love— but nothing is more complicated than organizing freedom. Rossi was persistent. "The family," he said, "has always been the largest breeding ground for immorality, wickedness, and stupidity."

The short story of the Cecília Colony ended after just four years. A century and a half later, its memory is still alive in anarchist daydreams. This adventure is steeped in melancholy. One has to wonder where this paradise went wrong to become a purgatory, and why it took the same rocky roads as most paradises, whether these were imagined by gods, heroes, myths, or men of good will.

What caused its failure? The colonists had to work like crazy. But at that time, an idea by French socialist Paul Lafargue had become popular among anarchists: *The Right to Be Lazy.*

For Giovanni Rossi the failure is due, above all, to the entanglements caused by free love.

Humanity was capable of creating small paradises: peaceful, happy communities without oppression or hierarchy, living in freedom and respect— once the poisons of bourgeois society had been eradicated.

"Free love has not yet penetrated the hearts of our companions, which causes a lot of trouble for those who are alone, although no one has ever been disrespectful to women."

One has to wonder where this paradise went wrong to become a purgatory, and why it took the same rocky roads as most paradises.

Plato, five centuries before our era, had already had to deal with this kind of shame. Admittedly, the model city in his *Laws* is far from being anarchic; on the contrary, he recommended the strictest of discipline. But Plato and Rossi pursued the same goal: to design the perfect society.

For Plato, if two young people wanted to have a child, a matron would watch over their amorous frolics as a way of preventing them from succumbing to any kind of sentiment, crude or uncontrolled behavior, or any kind of similar horrors. From the next day onward, both future parents would take their meals separately. Sitting in a canteen alongside everyone else! Some evenings there would be a ball and, joy of joys, boys and girls would appear naked. Not in their glad rags at all. The matrons would watch over them. The sole reason for this nudity was to match couples as best as possible, with the aim of furnishing the city with small citizens in their mold.

Plato targeted the family unit directly. Children would be taken from their parents as soon as they were born. Another danger then loomed. Fathers would run the risk of sleeping with their own daughters because they did not know who they were. But Plato had a remedy for that as well: every man would have to consider any girl born seven months after he made love to a woman to potentially be his daughter.

What is discouraging indeed is that Plato, the stormy theorist of the totalitarian city, and Giovanni Rossi, the apostle of anarchist happiness, propagated the same lesson: the family forms an infernal reef on which every floating paradise can run aground.

PHALANSTÈRE

Building a Paradise

———————

The nineteenth and twentieth centuries, as well as the eighteenth century, but let's not forget the fifteenth and sixteenth centuries, created many paradises (in the shape of convents, utopias, brothels, dazzling mansions, and courts of love). Generally speaking, these simply died out, gently, woefully, without even producing the romantic glow of an apocalypse.

Charles Fourier was one of those people who manufactured paradises. He was a brilliant man, both verbose and baroque. He invented the phalanstère (from the Greek *phalanx*, which designates a rectangular fortification, and *stereos*, which translates as "solid"). A medium-sized phalanstère

We endeavored to put workers' abodes inside a palace.

accommodated four hundred families (two thousand people) within a 988-acre (400 hectare) estate dedicated to growing flowers and vegetables.

One of Fourier's disciples, Jean-Baptiste André Godin, had made his fortune through the invention of cast-iron stoves. In his altruis-

tic nature, he created several practically designed, fair, and modern communities. The most famous was the Familistère de Guise. "Since we were unable to render each working-class family's garret a palace, we endeavored to put workers' abodes inside a palace." Godin was scolded for this approach by Karl Marx, who did not like his apparent bypassing of the "class struggle." Godin built another phalanstère in Brussels. Both communities were a success, though, strangely, both were dissolved in 1968.

However, the great revolts of the "beautiful month of May 1968" were the starting point of many utopian experiments. One of the most active of these is the Longo Maï Cooperatives in Limans, in the Alpes-de-Haute-Provence region of France, which was still in full swing as recently as 2017. The founders of this community had certainly taken precautions: Longo Maï, in Occitan, means "Long may it last."

"At Longo Maï we were protesters in 1970, and we are still protesters in 2017, with our free radio (Radio Zinzine), our chickens, our sheep, our tomatoes, our friends from all over the world, with or without papers, nomads, or settlers."

Lesquielles-
Saint-Germain

Oise

Guise

MILETUS

A Perfect, Deliberate, and Indestructible City

———

ASIA • 37°31' N, 16°45' E

Two thousand five hundred young wo-men busy themselves in a workshop, some sitting, others standing, almost all of them charming. The habit with which each worker executes the same task over and over again doubles the speed of her work and adds to its perfection. Several voices chanted a song full of grace and gusto about the pleasures of the workshop. The entire workshop repeated the chorus with charming gaiety.

—ÉTIENNE CABET

In the fifth century BCE, Greek cities flourished on the coast of Ionia, at the crossroads of Europe and Asia. These brought forward astounding developments. It was there, between Halicarnassus, Miletus, and Ephesus, on the edge of the Persian Empire, that the first notions of freedom were budding. These notions were still vague but already exuded a dazzling brilliance. They posited the first expressions of freedom, in opposition to the blind sentencing of the gods and the rules of blood.

Not far from there, on the other side of the Taurus Mountains, infinity and the realms of sand expand. How could the terrible rulers of Persia not covet the Greek cities of Ionia, full of mathematicians, poets, and dancers with auburn or purple hair, whose statues would be exhumed two thousand years later from the excavation site of the Parthenon?

Asian armies were getting closer. Miletus went on the offensive. The inhabitants burned down the city of Sardis, which Cyrus the Great had elected as the capital of the satrapy of Lydia. Darius the Great attacked. He turned Miletus into a field of ruins, but Miletus did not disappear from the map. The architect Hippodamus was tasked with rebuilding the devastated city. He was given carte blanche. So he invented a new model city.

Before Hippodamus, cities had developed by trial and error over millennia, in response to the upheavals of history. Among the building blocks for their houses were wood, stones, and sand, but also chaos, spontaneity, randomness, and unpredictability. The city was an organic formation just like sediment deposits, shells, moss, or forests.

Hippodamus was an innovator: his city would be deliberate, perfect, indestructible, and as strictly regulated as the constellations in the night sky. It would be exempt from the chaos of nature and history. Time, which is a factor of unrest, wars, and grief, would be expelled. The city, instead of slowly forming like a stalagmite, would suddenly emerge from Hippodamus's sketches and would immediately be complete, perfect, and definitive. It would be the love child of geometry and logic instead of the offspring of time and chance. It would not hesitate to violate the rules of geography if the necessities of mathematics, equality, or reason required it to do so.

Hippodamus was an architect. But he was also a philosopher. He was convinced that the design of a city, the network of its streets, the distribution of its neighborhoods and temples, and the location of its forum and its slaughterhouses would not only command the daily life of its inhabitants, their philosophy, and their desires, but also determine how the city would respond to the challenges of history. This new city, on this puzzling earth that humanity had received from the gods, would ensure the reign of logic and harmony. Amid the chaos there would be a small paradise of rationality.

Aristotle summarizes Hippodamus in a few lines: "The city of Hippodamus was composed of 10,000 citizens, divided into three parts—one of artisans, one of husbandmen, and a third of armed defenders of the state.

This new city, on this puzzling earth that humanity had received from the gods, would ensure the reign of logic and harmony.

He also divided the land into three parts: one sacred, one public, the third private" (*Politics*, translated by Benjamin Jowett).

Hippodamus bequeathed this square floor plan to his successors. His city is a work of geometry, with a network of streets intersecting at right angles. That was the Greek's coup de force. He tore the city from chaos to turn it into a network of lines, angles, and circles. He wrenched it from nature to replace the latter with an artifact, a "machinery" that would turn its inhabitants into a group of figures as perfect and immutable as the plans drawn with a ruler and compass.

The architect of Miletus was the inventor of a utopia: his city was based on calculations to ensure the harmony, peace, and happiness of its inhabitants. It drew the outlines of a paradise designed not by heroes or gods, but by engineers. Following in his footsteps, the Italian Tommaso Campanella, the Frenchmen Étienne Cabet and Charles Fourier, the Brits Francis Bacon and Thomas More, and dozens of geniuses penned their models of earthly paradise.

Like Hippodamus, they improved upon God's work. The Creator had certainly done a good job. He had some great ideas—for example, water, the sky, lions, or beetles—but he made all that very quickly, maybe with his eyes shut, and lost interest afterward. Even his masterpiece, this paradise amid a large garden, failed. It fell apart at the first misstep of humankind.

The utopians thus took over the relay. They would correct the gods' failed attempts. They would create all kinds of paradises.

Though these are not always the most inventive: in these perfect cities, there are no houris, nor snakes or devils, and not even a benevolent God. They do not promise to ward off evil, disease, and death. They are content with designing architecture, drawing up laws and contracts, and ensuring order, equality, justice, prosperity, and peace

The utopians thus took over the relay. They would correct the gods' failed attempts. They would create all kinds of paradises.

for the polis's citizens. In the absence of a genius, reason ruled the utopian city.

Hippodamus had countless disciples. They flocked to him. The cities they built were sometimes beautiful but always only temporary. One year, perhaps ten years of bliss, after which history came rushing back at the perfect city, and eternity shattered its dreams.

OCEANA

A Utopia Inspired by Reality

EUROPE • 45°26′ N, 12°19′ E

James Harrington was an English utopian of the seventeenth century, one of those men following in the footsteps of Plato—as people had been doing over the centuries—who would take pride in building ideal cities, paradises on Earth, and beautiful towns, and in creating infinite bliss.

Harrington did not hide the fact that his utopia, Oceana, was inspired by a real city: Venice. A wise choice. Venice, founded in 528, adopted a constitution in 1192; the head of their government was the doge, bound by the oath he made to the small Council of Trento and to three enduring social classes—the same as those proclaimed by Plato: the aristocrats, the guardians, and the people. This system would run without interruption, accident, or failure throughout the Middle Ages, the Renaissance, and the Enlightenment until Napoleon, a man of history instead of utopias, ended its prosperity in 1797. The same law and the same type of government had lasted for six centuries—a world record. Only the Vatican has lasted longer. Well . . .

Venice is a city of the sea. Built on 118 small islands, liquid space separates it from the eddies of time. This city seems otherworld-ly. A mysterious border divides it from other towns. It is like a mirage or an apparition: these waterways, these unreal bobbing gondolas, and the flickering of the open sea's salt water create an imaginary space. Palaces tremble in the waters' reflections. Their image is upset and settles again following the storms and the calm of the sea. It is a city of borders and a city behind the mirrors.

Without going so far as to banish death, which ravaged as it pleased, the utopians at least tried to reduce the unpleasant surprises of time passing and the misdeeds of history.

Like Atlantis, this city of the sea corrects the work of nature. In these confines, geography fails and technology comes to its aid. A paradise of bridges and roads envelops it that consists of nothing but artifice: valves, locks, gears and pulleys, viaducts and endless screws, bridges, cogs, and sprockets. Eight rivers were diverted. Hills were remod-

eled. Sandy spits were created, correcting the vanishing points and changing the color of the horizons. The Venetians improved those sketches lazily drawn by the Creator. They submitted geographical drafts to the rigorous scrutiny of mathematicians and craftspeople. And while they were at it, they turned their city into a little paradise, certainly less dazzling than that mentioned in Genesis, but of a more rational kind, more technological and less puritan.

The Venetians were aware that they had created a masterpiece. They were working hard to control access to it. Like all utopias, all paradises, Venice was allergic to immigrants. It wanted to retain its pleasures for its own children alone. Every stranger equaled a microbe that must be stopped at the border. Immigration levels: almost zero. Breaking into Venice was not easy. The Piombi, the fierce prison located in the attic of the doge's palace, existed to put off intruders. These precautions and dungeons allowed La Serenissima to survive the convulsions of the late Middle Ages, the chaos of the Renaissance, and the revolutions of early modernity without having to adjust its regulations and without succumbing.

Nothing ever had to change in this sublime city. The constitution of 1192 provided that each new generation would replace the preceding one without progress or decline. In short: it would remain the same. No one could change their social class or improve upon it.

Admittedly, this rule was sometimes broken: no paradise is perfect, and it happens that time itself has an effect, even on Eden. The doges continually tried to block its path and to reconcile movement and immobility, time, and the absence of time. They obeyed the laws of water and wind. The sea is always in motion: it makes waves and creates storms or periods of stillness, yet it never changes. And that is what Venice is like: La Serenissima is shaken by the tempests of history and yet it persists.

Could it be that Venice is only a dazzling trompe l'oeil, a painted canvas concealing the arsenal and bombardments, the warrior galleys and heroic sailors who saved Europe on October 7, 1571, in the Battle of Lepanto, from the attack of the Ottoman Empire, and whose rich traders allowed this utopia to travel unscathed throughout centuries and the hubbub of wars?

This unique positioning explains the relationship that Venice has with its artists. The

Between history—in which sailors, soldiers, and the merchants of Venice play their parts—and a utopia—reflected here and there throughout the centuries—where is the secret hiding place of Venice's paradise?

city of the doges has its own history of art, which differs from that of the rest of Europe. It does not care about "modernism" and has a disdain for successive "schools." Whenever an old mosaic shattered into pieces, the Roman procurators of Venice ensured that it was restored to such high standards that no one could spot the difference. One day, Titian proposed to create new mosaics for St. Mark's Basilica. The procurators thought about it. The verdict was passed in 1566: we are getting along just fine without the genius of Titian. They preferred to faithfully restore the old masterpieces. Time passing and things changing are not popular in Venice. At the end of the sixteenth century, a fire ravaged the doge's palace. Star architect Andrea Palladio proposed to build another one. The offer was rejected: instead, the original plans were dug out from the darkest corner of the city archives and followed to a T.

What is real and what is illusion in this lush stage set governed by shadows and the sea? Venice is the stage of a fabulous opera whose backdrop is made up of a string of islands and gondolas that glide without making a wave. Between history—in which sailors, soldiers, and the merchants of Venice play their parts—and a utopia—reflected here and there throughout the centuries—where is the secret hiding place of Venice's paradise? Is it the formidable net that the doges have cast onto history to submit it to their whims and desires? Is it the carnival that leads women, their faces embellished with ash, gold, and gemstones, to turn like automatons of death?

THE SEA

ISLANDS OF WOMEN

The Art of Evasion

ASIA • 12°31' N, 53°55' E

Since the beginning of time, islands have been in motion. They are submerged by the sea and reemerge at the ocean's surface. One day they appear out in the sun or the mist, just to return to their night and the unknown. There is an explanation for these wandering whims. Although the sailors of ancient times knew how to calculate latitudes, they were unable to determine longitudes. That's why they never knew exactly where they were. They would sail blindly, and if they came across an island they would randomly drop a pin on their world map, meaning that the same reef could be discovered four or five times. On maps, the same island could have multiple names. It could occupy several spots, sometimes hundreds of nautical miles apart. It was not until the eighteenth century and the invention of sophisticated nautical clocks that sailors knew which distant seas they were navigating. These days, the abominable GPS has dealt a blow to the poetry of the journey, but, thank goodness, sailors are stubborn and their boats continue to come across fleeting islands. These islands, whenever they appear in the muggy parts of the equator, look like earthly paradises. They are abundant with flowers, fruit, fish, and hummingbirds. Their beaches sparkle under the azure double act of the sea and the sky. They will forever be at the heart of things, enveloped in empty space and an almost-void. Of the vastness of the universe, they only know the stars and the perfect circle of the horizon. Like many paradises, they form a landscape that is both minute and infinite. It is easy to see why they would have awakened navigators' desire. Safeguarded by their remoteness, the sea, and their uniqueness, they offered sailors a rare opportunity to disembark in a place free from constraints, chains, regulations, and religious rules without police and the virtues that pollute cities. There, the foolishness of priests and the wickedness of princes no longer prevail. All principles taught on land wither, first and foremost those sexual mores detested by sailors. That is why the ancient maps of the world are full of islands that are, as a preference, populated by women only.

The Islands of Women are in the Southern Hemisphere, because apparently all the principles that govern northern societies are reversed as soon as one crosses the equator. This anomaly was well known to the ancient

68

Greeks: the sin of lust had never successfully gained a foothold in southern countries.

Portuguese sailors and soldiers who arrived in Brazil made hay of this curious rule. They saw naked women on the beaches and in the trees. They caught them and made love to them, and everyone was happy. Moreover, a high ecclesiastical authority had endorsed this privilege: *Ultra aequinoctialem nao pecari*: "There is no sin south of the equator," decreed Caspar Van Baleus, chaplain to Maurice of Nassau, the governor of Recife. All Brazilians, even those who do not know Latin, would cite this encouraging formula at the drop of a hat.

In the twelfth century, Marco Polo spotted an island inhabited only by women in the Ethiopian Sea. It would change location now and then, but you could generally reach it by sailing south as you were coming from Makran, India. Islands of Women were also known in America. John Mandeville reported a very large one in his fantastical *Travels of Sir John Mandeville*. It seems it's quite easy to get there: you just have to "go beyond Chaldea and reach the Amazon." You would then be welcomed into the "Land of Feminine," full of Amazons with cut breasts. Unfortunately, Mandeville lived two centuries before Brazil was discovered.

In 1439, another women's island was discovered near the island of Socotra, in the Indian Ocean. Even Christopher Columbus was looking for a paradise of women in 1493, when he returned from the Caribbean Sea. The Native Americans he had taken on board were guiding him, but they muddled up their calculations and missed this paradise.

With the exception of the land of the Amazons, which was guided by particular rules, most of these islands were alike. Women would live there among themselves but accepted that men entered their kingdom for a few days or weeks. That was just as well, because European sailors would make rather brief stopovers anyway. When they landed they were not idle, and they quickly bid farewell again.

All these paradises, which God had the wisdom to plant all across the globe, have the same drawback, however: they are not easy to find. The routes leading there remain uncertain and complicated, and the directions are contradictory. At times it would seem as if these islands resembled the women who inhabited them: the art of evasion was part of their genius and the secret of their allure. Sailors eventually lost hope. Instead they thought up small artificial paradises reserved for their sole pleasure.

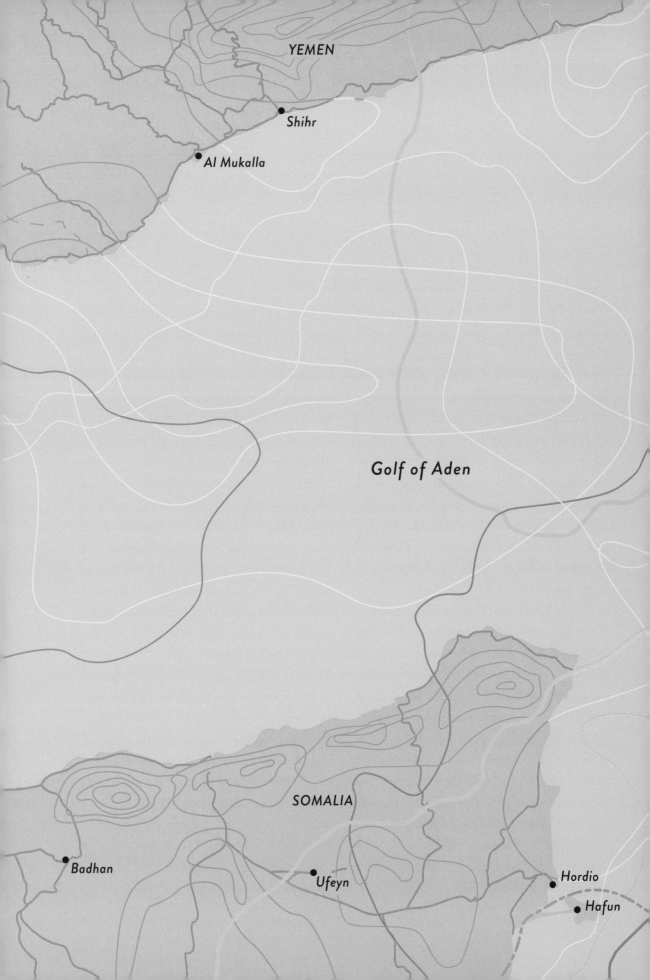

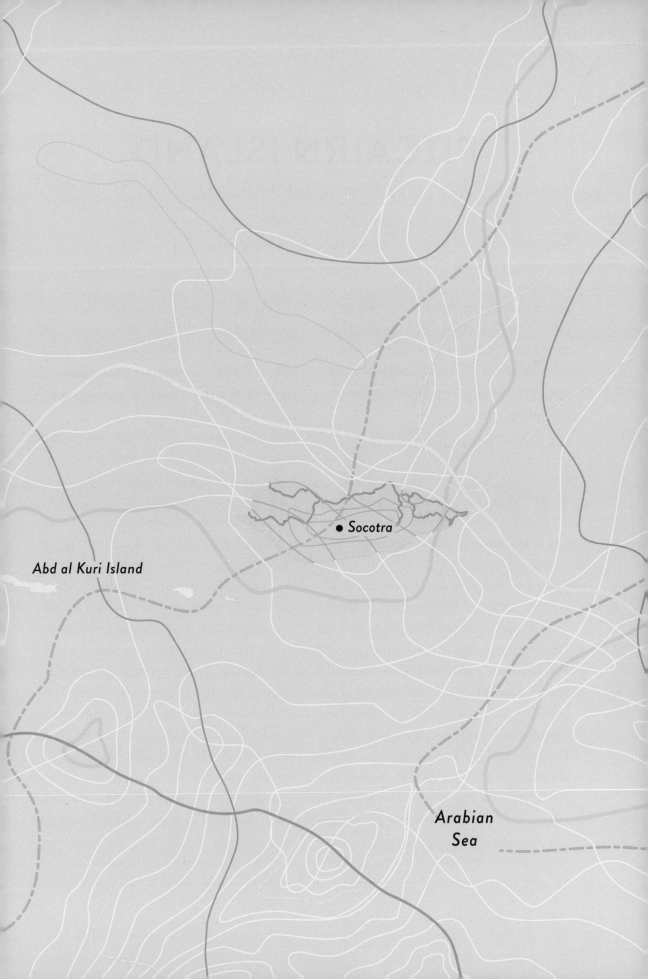

Abd al Kuri Island

● Socotra

Arabian
Sea

PITCAIRN ISLAND

The Mutineers of the Bounty

OCEANIA • 25°00' S, 130°00' W

After I had been there about ten or twelve days, it came into my thoughts that I should lose my reckoning of time for want of books, and pen and ink, and should even forget the Sabbath days.

—ROBINSON CRUSOÉ by Daniel Defoe

Her Majesty's ship the *Bounty* dropped anchor in Tahiti in April 1789. The plan was to fill the hold with breadfruit trees to deliver to Jamaica, but that never happened because a mutiny broke out on board. The master's mate, Fletcher Christian, seized the ship, threw Captain William Bligh into the 26-foot-long (8 meter) open launch, wished him godspeed, and set sail. Thus begins the most famous naval mutiny. Hollywood has turned it into masterpieces starring Gary Cooper, Clark Gable, and Marlon Brando.

The wild crew had two aims: to escape the inhumane rule governing ships at that time and to found a new society in a secret location, unlike any other kind of community humanity had ever conceived. A few years earlier, Louis Antoine de Bougainville thought he had happened upon paradise in the Pacific islands. His unlikely successor, Fletcher Christian, had more-ambitious plans yet. Since even "good savages" could be "bad," Christian and his crew wanted to settle on an unadulterated island and create their own New Cythera.

Nothing happened for a long time afterward. One might have thought that Christian's undertaking had not gone to plan. Yet, there, surrounded by the vastness of infinity and under the watchful eyes of the ocean, an unparalleled society had flourished: happy, fair, and protected from the turmoil of history—at the very moment the bloodbaths of the French Revolution, then caused by Napoleon's soldiers, were washing over Europe. New Cythera, serenaded by poets for so long, had finally transcended the realm of dreams. Paradise had become a possibility. And since it was hidden and impossible to track down, paradise had the slightest chance to escape the messy twists of fate brought on by the human condition.

Of course this recovery of Eden came at a price. Fletcher Christian paid it in full by committing a terrible act, the most heinous of crimes, when he refused to obey his superior's orders; that is, the order estab-

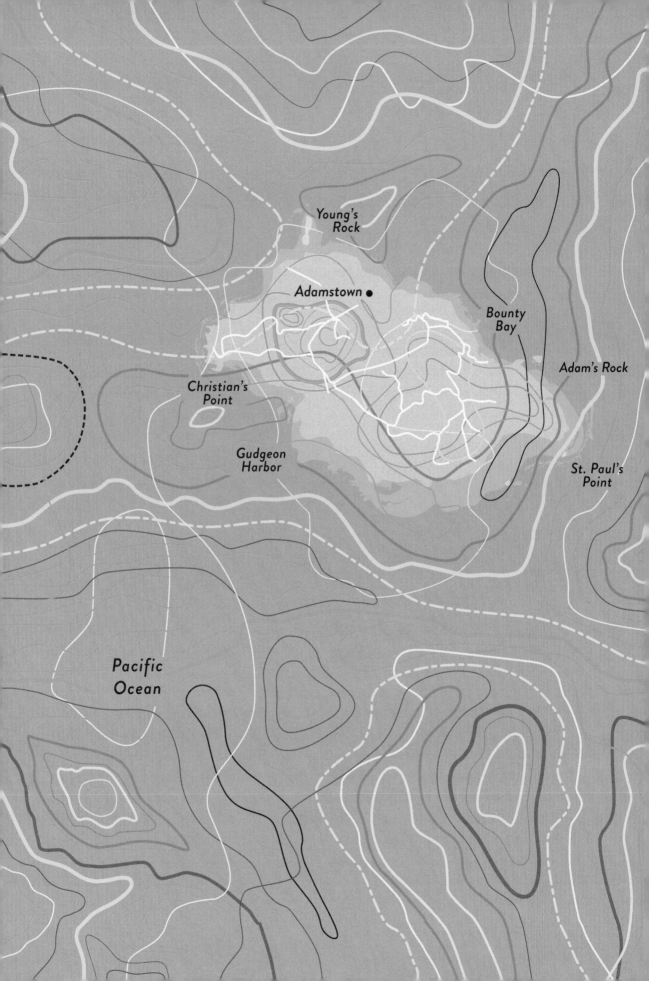

Young's
Rock

Adamstown ●

Bounty
Bay

Adam's Rock

Christian's
Point

St. Paul's
Point

Gudgeon
Harbor

Pacific
Ocean

lished by the laws of history, by his nation, and by tradition.

Should this have come as a surprise? To reopen the gates of the Enchanted Garden, Christian had to commit the worst of sacrileges: a naval mutiny. It was on this condi-

To reopen the gates of the Enchanted Garden, Christian had to commit the worst of sacrileges: a naval mutiny.

tion alone that the wild sailors were capable of rejecting the faded finery of civilization in the waters around Tahiti.

In 1818 an American captain discovered, by chance, on the small Pitcairn Island a tiny English colony whose existence had hitherto been unknown. The last survivor of the *Bounty*, Alexander Smith, who was actually called John Adams, still lived there with a few descendants of the mutineers. A little later, in 1825, the British Admiralty launched a new expedition with the mission to file a report on Pitcairn Island and its cu-

rious colony. John Adams was still there. They reassured him: he would not be prosecuted as long as he recounted his memories and made his notebook available, telling the story of the survival of the mutineers of the *Bounty* on Pitcairn Island. This text was astounding: readers would expect happiness, love, and freedom. But in fact they encountered an account of hell.

In the beginning, in 1789, when the mutineers of the *Bounty* landed on Pitcairn Island, everything was still going splendidly in the best of all possible worlds. The island was as pleasant as if it had just been formed by the hands of the Creator. There was water aplenty, forests, and fruit. The mutineers of the *Bounty*, who had taken the precaution of bringing male and female Tahitians with them, were in good spirits.

They went on to divide the land. That was their first mistake, because the lands of the Lord belong to everyone and must not be split into private property (Bakunin, who was not alive yet, would put it well). Worse still: each sailor received a plot of land, but the Black Polynesians were left empty-handed. Think about it: the Black people were slaves, so what use would they have for property?

Two years passed. One day, Adams's wife is collecting eggs on top of a cliff.

She slips and falls to her death. Her husband is furious and demands that he be provided with another wife. He forces one of the Black slaves to hand over his own wife. The Black men thus decide to attack the whites and snuff them out. But the Black women pass over to the enemy. They warn the white people by singing a lament: "Why is the Black man sharpening his ax? It's to kill the white man."

The white people get the hint and bring the Black people back under their control. But this return to order does not go down well. People start killing each other willy-nilly. One of the Black people is shot by his own nephew. Another perishes under the combined blows of his best friend and his own wife. That's always the thing with chaos: it is attracted to paradise. Whenever chaos discovers a Garden of Eden and manages to sneak in, it wreaks havoc. One morning the leader of the mutineers of the *Bounty*, Fletcher Christian, goes out to hoe the yams in his small garden. He is killed by four men. The widows of murdered white men join forces to kill the last Black people. They miss their goal.

Revolting Black women hide the skulls of five murdered white men. The white people re-claim these skulls to provide a dignified burial for their brothers. This irritates the women, and they hatch a plan. They are going to kill all the white people in their sleep. Evil is rampant.

Everything was still going splendidly in the best of all possible worlds. The island was as pleasant as if it had just been formed by the hands of the Creator.

Among the last survivors is MacCoy, of Scottish origin. He fashions himself a still to produce whiskey. Since he has taken a liking to drink, he suffers from "delirium tremens." In his state, he climbs on top of a very high rock and attempts to fly away—but falls to his death. By this point there are only two survivors left of the *Bounty* mutineers: Adams and Young. They both are very pious and say their prayers each morning and evening. But Young suffers a ferocious asthma attack and suffocates. Adams and the children of the former mutineers are all that remain. Paradise does not need to close its gates. It never opened them.

ATLANTIS

The Most Splendid of Paradises

EUROPE • 28°06′ N, 15°24′ W

For us, the free space of the sea, not ordinary men, blinded by domestic stars.

—Saint-John Perse

Atlantis is a marvel. Of all the paradises recorded to date, this is the most splendid. It lay beyond the Pillars of Hercules, in the high seas of the ocean. Its land, lapped by the waves, was abundant with all that nature has to offer. Elephants populated its grasslands, as did squirrels and all of God's creatures. The countryside was full of pleasant scents. The cities, built in white, red, and black stone, sparkled with the beauty of traditional mosaics of the Barbary Coast.

Atlantis consisted of five concentric circles of land separated by rings of water. Its governors were descendants of the Titan Atlas, son of Poseidon, whose daughters were the guardians of the golden apples of the Garden of the Hesperides—probably in the Canary Islands—the so-called Atlantides or Pleiades. At the center stood a monument of ivory and metal, the Temple of Poseidon, the god of the sea, whose carriage is drawn by horses with golden manes. On a stele were etched the laws of Atlantis. This is where priests sacrificed holy bulls.

On this immense labyrinth of sea, sky, gold, and earth, very sophisticated engineers built vertiginous structures, bridges, locks, underground pools, canals, turrets, interchanges, tunnels, and ports.

Vast fleets floated on the canals, since the Atlanteans were seafarers and merchants.

Atlantis is a marvel. Of all the paradises recorded to date, this is the most splendid.

In the silky softness of the twilight, young, elegant people would be dancing, scantily dressed in tulles and voile, floating tunics, and satin robes studded with tourmalines and opals. The gods peppered their paradise with a metal that we have long since forgotten: orichalcum, which is almost as precious as gold and resembles fire. Which mortal would not want to possess even just a small quantity of orichalcum? Which fiancée would not risk selling her soul to the devil for a few carats of orichalcum?

76

Atlantic
Ocean

● Arrecife
Lanzarote

La Palma

● Puerto
del Rosario

● Santa Cruz

Tenerife

● Las Palmas

Fuerteventura

La Gomera

Gran Canaria

El Hierro

Western
Sahara

Many people would quite like to take a little trip to these sumptuous lands, but how to get there? Plato never even saw Atlantis, which did not diminish his reputation, because finding a land that no one can see requires a great deal of genius. Moreover, there is an excuse for Plato's incompetence in this regard: Atlantis was swallowed up by the sea thirteen millennia ago; that is to say, nine thousand years before Plato disclosed its secret.

On a fateful Day of Wrath, the large island sank to the bottom of the muddy sea.

He cites his sources: a long time ago, Egyptian priests spoke about Atlantis to another Greek philosopher, Solon. Subsequently this information was passed on from one philosopher to the next, until it eventually reached Plato.

Like so many other paradises, this one did not hold up and ended up vanishing. Pla-to tells us how it sank. Its prosperity and abundance of wonders, its streams of precious stones, and its pretty and voluptuous women: all that aroused envy and jealousy. All bedlam had broken loose among the society of Greek gods. Zeus, who never liked his brother Poseidon anyway, was afraid that the Atlantides would have illusions of grandeur and forget the principles of wisdom and modesty.

So he put an end to the adventure. He proceeded with a rare degree of brutality. In one single night, an earthquake shook Atlantis to the core. And since Zeus was quite impulsive, he added four floods to this misfortune. On a fateful Day of Wrath, the large island sank to the bottom of the muddy sea. But mourning was not in Atlantis's nature. It let a few centuries pass after Plato died to reemerge from its abyss and begin its long afterlife.

Atlantis had never been more active than since it had disappeared. Instead of stagnating in its azure eternity, it bounced back and migrated. It became nomadic. It traveled around all four cardinal points, between the Levant and the Atlantic Ocean, between the Southern Lands and the North.

The Canary Islands were a popular destination. These consist of seven islands, which gives them an advantage since seven is a

Its prosperity and abundance of wonders, its streams of precious stones, and its pretty and voluptuous women: all that aroused envy and jealousy.

sacred number. In ancient times they were famous because they were regarded as the location of the Garden of the Hesperides. Hercules knew this garden well. He had completed one of his tasks there, the eleventh, by picking the golden fruit from an apple tree, but the Hesperides fell into oblivion since. No one remembered where they had gone. It was not until 1402 when a Norman sailor, Jean de Béthencourt, rediscovered them in the shape of the Canaries. He received a kind welcome from the people of Guanches—the Atlanteans for sure.

Naturalist Georges Cuvier, in the nineteenth century, speculated that nine thousand years ago the natural dam of the Bosphorus, which is situated on the Eurasian tectonic fault line, collapsed, causing a flood. Nine thousand years ago . . . that coincides with the time Atlantis sank to the bottom of the sea. It also left its marks on Gibraltar, not far from the Atlas Mountains, which bear the name of the first king of Atlantis. Recent speculations have stated that Atlantis took advantage of the flood to cross the ocean and dock in Rio de Janeiro, on a huge rock named Pedra da Gávea, which looks like one of the Atlantes and features Phoenician graffiti.

Bible scholars have confirmed that some Atlantes had sneaked into Jericho, which caused the wrath of the heavens and all the trials and tribulations listed in the Bible. And the alchemists who ran shops in Prague's Golden Lane understood that orichalcum, this fire-like metal that was abundant in Atlantis, must be the philosopher's stone that they hoped to collect in their stills.

THE REPUBLIC OF PIRATES

Escaping the Boredom of Paradise

SOUTH AMERICA • 17°56' N, 76°50' W

All they [the pirates] take is equally divided, as hath been said before: yea, they take a solemn oath to each other, not to conceal the least thing they find among the prizes; and if any one is found false to the said oath, he is immediately turned out of the society. They are very civil and charitable to each other; so that if any one wants what another has, with great willingness they give it one to another.

—ALEXANDRE OLIVIER EXMELIN (translated by George Alfred Williams)

Pirates are never satisfied. They do not understand why they have been expelled from paradise before even entering it. Before even emitting their first cry as a baby, they were already tarnished with evil, had already committed an appalling sin, and were being punished for it. This predetermination enrages them. So they reject it. Abbots and the pope try to appease them, advising them to let a few million years pass, after which everything will be back to normal because the Second Coming will save them all. But pirates have a stormy temper. And they are greedy. They want their paradise right away.

So they bid farewell to their parents, to their Sussex or Normandy villages, and run to the shore. They storm one of the king's ships and sail for Eden. This Eden changes location over the centuries but always hides in warmer regions, not far from the equator: in the seventeenth century, for example, it was in the Caribbean (Turtle Island, Santo Domingo, Jamaica, Haiti, etc.), whereas in the following century it was to be found in the Indian Ocean, near Madagascar. There are islands well hidden in the folds of the vast blue sea and packed to the brim with all the ingredients of a paradise: bananas and sweet potatoes, plenty of freedom, cassava, wild pigs, idleness, rabbits, colorful birds, sunshine, and women.

The police states of old Europe have not yet come to civilize these isolated places. There are no soldiers and no police officers. Instead, infinite freedom. The inventions of civilization have not yet taken root here.

Santa Clara

Atlantic
Ocean

CUBA

Las Tunas

JAMAICA

Kingston

Caribbean
Sea

No judges or prisons. No boundary markings or title deeds. No archive either, except those of the wind. Not even original sin. Every morning the world is born anew. No ancestors, no children, no yesterday, and no tomorrow. There, at the edge of the world, in the perpetual cycle of night and day, the pirate drops his kit in the sand. He tells himself that he has reached paradise.

Every morning the world is born anew. No ancestors, no children, no yesterday, and no tomorrow.

Unfortunately, paradise has the same disadvantages as eternity: it's the same old, same old. After a little while, even here time seems to expand. As pleasant, lively, and fun as a new paradise is, as boring an old one can get. It keeps repeating the same things. So the pirates are moping around in their Eden. They go on strolls under the coconut palms, eat a few wild pigs, and caress women, but they soon run out of ideas for what to do with all these breasts, all these barbecues, all these naps. They end up doing what the Creator once did to others: they curse themselves and banish themselves from paradise. They return to the beach, prepare their old tubs, rush to the edge of the world, and enlist the devil in their crew.

Captain Lewis, who sailed out of Port Royal—the most immoral city of his time—had pledged allegiance to the devil. He would not take a single decision without consulting Beelzebub, Satan, or the Grim Reaper. And he was driven by bloodlust. His ship would prowl across the seven seas like a wolf. To prove to his crew that he was the son of darkness, he announced to his sailors the predicted time of his death. And he died precisely at that time.

Captain Fly was no better. He captured a royal officer. That man cried out and wanted to say his last prayer. Fly was outraged: "God damn you! Since you are so devilishly pious, we will
give you time to say your prayers. I will be your pastor." Then he would say a funeral valediction, laugh, and massacre his captive.

Another one of Satan's accomplices was Captain Teach. He took a few of his sailors and locked himself into the hold of his ship to randomly fire into the dark, simply because he wanted to show that he did not need a grudge or reason to injure or kill. He claimed to be acting in the name of Satan. When asked where he had hidden his treasures, he replied, "Only I and the devil know. And in the end, the devil will have the whole lot."

One of Captain Roberts's sailors, a certain Sutton, was taken to the gallows. Another man awaiting the same end was praying:

"Where do you think all these prayers will get you?"

"Heaven."

"Heaven? Are you mad? Have you ever heard of a pirate going to heaven? I want to be in hell. It's much more pleasant than in heaven, and as soon as I get there, I'll greet Captain Roberts with thirteen salutes."

Another sailor from Roberts's crew shared this philosophy: "We laugh at the king, his parliament, and his pardons. We are even less afraid of the gallows. If we are defeated

That was the fate of the pirates. They had embarked for the promised land to pitch their tent in the Garden of Earthly Delights and ended up in the clutches of the devil.

or ambushed, we will ignite the powders and go to hell cheerfully and in good company." That was the fate of the pirates. They had embarked for the promised land to pitch their tent in the Garden of Earthly Delights and ended up in the clutches of the devil. "Paradise or hell, what does it matter?" They relished the beauty of things for a few seasons only, before dying without having found fame or fortune. Their bones were returned to the sands and their memory is etched in the calligraphy of the void.

SAINT BRENDAN'S ISLAND

Paradise Was a Whale

———————

EUROPE • 28°06' N, 15°24' W

Saint Brendan was a very pious ancient Irish monk. He had his mind fervently set on discovering paradise, so he asked his abbey for a sabbatical and built a boat from stretched cattle hides. In it he placed provisions and a couple of monks. And off they went! In 530 CE he found a paradise and returned to Ireland. He then published the account of his travels and his discovery.

One day, Saint Brendan's dingy drops anchor. The monks think that this piece of land must be paradise, since islands lend themselves to bliss. The monks disembark. They make a fire to prepare a meal but at that moment the island begins to shake.

The text was a great hit and became "cult." Beginning in the eighth century, many versions of the voyage of Saint Brendan circulated in Europe. Albeit exciting, these texts were vague. Some of them situated Eden in the vicinity of the Canary Islands. Others moved it into the snow, 485 miles (780 kilometers) northwest of Ireland, possibly to America.

In the thirteenth century, another monk, a certain Benedict, published *Navigatio Sancti Brendani abbatis* and set things straight: one day, Saint Brendan's dingy drops anchor near a small island. The monks think that this piece of land must be paradise, since islands lend themselves to bliss. The monks disembark. They make a fire to prepare a meal, but at that moment the island begins to shake. It jumps and jerks, twists and turns. The monks get scared. They call Saint Brendan to the rescue, who has stayed behind on board. They tell him, "Hey, abbot, our master, wait for us, for the whole earth is set in motion." From this story the interpreters of the account concluded that paradise must be a whale.

Norwegian
Sea

ICELAND

Vatnajökull
National Park

Reykjavik

Faroe Islands

Glasgow

Atlantic
Ocean

IRELAND

Dublin

NEW CYTHERA

A Land without Sin or Misfortune

———◆———

It is not without reason that we look towards the south to seek happiness. An ancient memory drives us there, and a recognition renders us happy at the edge of the South Sea. These are the baths of the Tertiary period. The world inhabits man with its history and prehistory; within man reside the labyrinth and the sphinx that questions him.

—ERNST JÜNGER

That was the time when Europeans found paradise. They equipped ships in Southampton, Nantes, London, La Rochelle, and Saint-Malo and sailed for Cape Horn. There they navigated around reefs and through storms, and sometimes got shipwrecked, but they said that paradise was worth it. Those who managed to survive discovered vast blue seas. A topman would spot an island here and there. Clinging on to the mast, he would announce the good news, and the sailors would start to get excited because nothing lends itself more to being a paradise than an island, provided that it be distant and hard to find, and that its remoteness meant it had been spared history's filthy marks.

In 1756 a paradise emerged from the shadows. Frenchman Louis Antoine de Bougainville came across the island of Tahiti, which a British sailor, Samuel Wallis, had happened upon a few months earlier, without realizing that he was at the gates of paradise. Bougainville was better educated in these matters—and pushed open the gates. "I thought I was transported to the Garden of Eden." He lists the delights of the place: the climate is perfect, mild, and stable; the landscapes elegant; and the trees often unknown and beautiful. The island has not been disfigured by volcanoes—the jaws of hell that are so common in the tropics. No snakes and no venomous mosquitoes. Tahitians, especially the women, are elegant and tall. They swim gracefully and have beautiful hair. They live in a harmonious society: strict equality, unfettered freedom, and peace.

Upon his return to Europe, Bougainville noted all this down in a book, *A Voyage around the World*. It became an immediate success. A divine surprise: on the other side of the world, humanity had finally spotted the "good savage,"

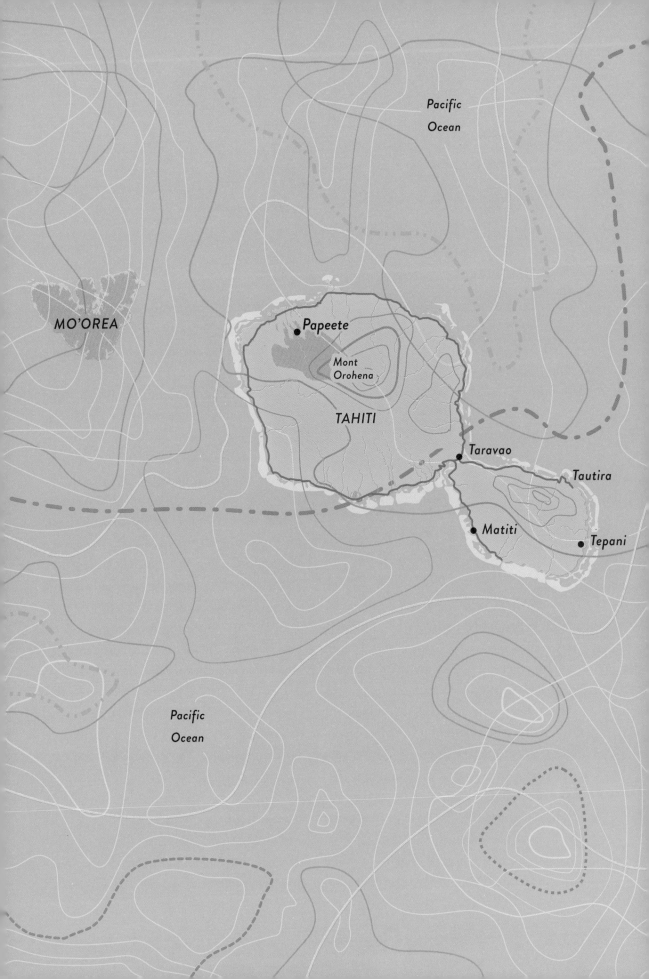

MO'OREA

Pacific
Ocean

Papeete

Mont
Orohena

TAHITI

Taravao

Tautira

Matiti

Tepani

Pacific
Ocean

the one Jean-Jacques Rousseau had described but that no one had ever encountered. Bougainville baptized the large island "New Cythera."

Nothing lends itself more to being a paradise than an island, provided that it be distant and hard to find, and that its remoteness meant it had been spared history's filthy marks.

The name was well chosen. The Enlightenment adored ancient Greece, and Cythera had been in fashion ever since Antoine Watteau had painted a *Pilgrimage to Cythera*. Once upon a time, in Greek mythology, the island of Kythira housed a temple dedicated to Aphrodite, the goddess of love, who had emerged from the surrounding waves. Watteau painted this island and placed the statue of Aphrodite on the edge of a forest with abundant foliage.

The skies are blue and pink. A string of young people are advancing toward the shore, but Watteau is not showing us whether they are disembarking or leaving the island of love. The painting is veiled in a golden air of melancholy. The look on the women's faces suggests that they are leaving. Several are looking back as if they were saying farewell to the land without sin or misfortune.

Another detail is surprising: unlike the protocols that stifled the regulated societies of Europe at that time, the men whom Watteau paints do not need to showcase their talents for their companions to fall into their trap. The women cling to them, a bit like, fifty years later, the sailors of *La Boudeuse* and *L'Étoile*, who do not have to be on their best behavior to seduce the ravishing ladies of New Cythera. They would rush to their dugouts laden with women and flowers.

Bougainville's crews dropped anchor on the edge of a new Cythera. The sailors were enchanted by the curious ways of the young Tahitian women. These were the ways of paradise. Love, far from being forbidden or condemned, is not a source of shame here. It is tender and pure. Women at the end of the world didn't care about sin—

they had never even heard of it, thank goodness! They liked caresses and enjoyed themselves, and that was that. While the women of Europe would play-act and pinch pennies, the ladies of New Cythera did not need much encouragement. They enjoyed making love. And they didn't understand why they should charge for the pleasure they were getting from the seafarers' bodies.

Like that of Watteau, Bougainville's paradise was fragile. It did not take much to upset it. Eight days passed and their luck had run out. A society without hatred or villainy, without money and mischief, revealed its depravity. The sailors witnessed a couple of brawls. The good savages would lie just as much as bad civilized people did. They committed acts of fraud and pillaged a little. There were a few deaths.

The Europeans discovered that this society, apparently without violence and oppression, also waged war, slayed its enemies, and happily devoured them. More disappointing yet: the bodies of these young women who had at first given themselves freely and without malicious intent quickly became market goods, a currency. The daughters of New Cythera, perhaps encouraged by their companions, suddenly asked for payment. And they had found the ideal currency: they demanded that their lovers pay them in nails, a commodity more precious than gold, since Tahiti, barely out of the golden age at this point, was still ignorant about blacksmithing.

When Captain Wallis raised his anchor after a few weeks in the Tahitian paradise, he realized that his ship was not working properly anymore. It had been dismantled, bit by bit, since all the iron nails that had supported the masts and the hatches had been used to pay for the bodies of those young women without malicious intent or sin.

Their luck had run out. In a flash, and thanks to a trade in bodies, paradise had closed up shop. The unadulterated island had entered the Iron Age, and all the plagues of Western societies had depreciated it. New Cythera died at the same time as it discovered the rule of supply and demand, modesty, the impurity of the flesh, the misappropriation of public funds, jealousy and corruption, and the rule of banks. As Genesis would have it, women's bodies play a role in these misfortunes. Pleasure, desire, and innocence bear the markers of infamy. The time of innocence has come to an end. The paradise of the beginning of time has given way to savages devoted to sin, money, and death.

THE *MAYFLOWER*

A Cape on Innocent Land

Two dangers constantly threaten the world: order and disorder.

—PAUL VALÉRY (translated by Stuart Gilbert)

On September 16, 1620, a three-master set sail from Plymouth, England. It had about one hundred passengers on board. A century had passed since Christopher Columbus, but the New World was still unspoiled. This encouraged these pilgrims, since they had no small ambition: they wanted to move to paradise.

It must be said that, as far as paradise was concerned, Europe had failed. This continent was a melting pot of witches, villains, scorpions, ruffians, and corrupt people. People would dismember their enemies, strip them to their bones, and imprison, burn, and torture them, all in the name of God. Kings, common men, and the clergy had turned the land of God into the land of the devil. The passengers of the *Mayflower* had experienced it themselves: since they belonged to a Puritan sect, the king of England, James VI and I, persecuted them with a vengeance.

Thank God the pilgrims had set sail for innocent lands. There, westward ho, protected by the winds and the sea, was America, untouched by sin, felonies, misfortune, and corruption. Onward to Eden! The pilgrims were fleeing the villainy of the Old World. This land of Canaan that humanity had been looking for since Abraham's days and that was thought to be lost was awaiting them. Columbus was not wrong: early America featured many paradisaical parts. Virginia was a paradise, Maryland a garden of delights, and Georgia an Eden. As for Massachusetts, where the *Mayflower* landed, "It is the place where the Lord will create a new heavens and a new earth." A new era would begin here.

Back in England, Thomas Hooker, paraphrased by George Steiner, confirmed that New England was "a signal of the end of secular time. . . . Any ulterior discovery and instauration would . . . herald the beginning of the reign of everlastingness as foretold in Revelation." America was a piece of the original Garden of Eden set aside to welcome the newborn Adam.

Here began the reign of the new man, cleansed from all his sins, far removed from the men who die year in, year out.

"For we must consider that we shall be as a city upon a hill," said John Winthrop. "The eyes of all people are upon us. So that if we shall deal falsely with our God in this work we have undertaken, and so cause Him to withdraw His present help from us, we shall be made a story and a byword through the world."

Far from the horrors of history, Massachusetts was the "land of Canaan." He put Adam and the Adamites back in the saddle. "Thus New England," wrote George Steiner, "was not only the precise analogue to the Promised Land, but the Noah's ark in a period of deluge." The Puritans, therefore, had to be prepared for swells and sudden pitches, but the children of Abraham were experienced: had they not, too, wandered through frightening deserts and suffered sorrow and hurt on their march for Canaan?

Nowadays we may wonder whether the *Mayflower* pilgrims might not have been a little mistaken when they thought they could just pitch their tents in the land of Canaan and reopen the gates of paradise on Earth. In the days of the "Pilgrim Fathers," one man asked himself precisely that question. This man was Thomas Morton. While John Winthrop's friends founded the Adamic Plymouth Colony, Morton belonged to the colony of Merrymount. The Adamic members of the Plymouth Colony would vilify him. He also celebrated the beginning of a new era, but in his own way: he would organize huge orgies with plenty of naked Adams and Eves. But his gravest sin was something else: instead of "knowing," like his peers in Plymouth, that Native Americans were not the children of God and could not apply for the role of new Adam, Morton entertained very friendly relationships with the locals. Furthermore, he crossed the boundary of ethnicity by making love to native women. And he could not even be cast away into the dark pits of hell by labeling him a "pagan," because he professed his faith in God! He even dared to compare himself to the Canaanites, to the very people who had been driven out of Eden by the Israelites. Morton loved sex and parties, God and sensuality, joy and freedom. He reminds us of François Rabelais, who, a century earlier, had opposed the appalling "hygienic paradise" of the island of Utopia as imagined by Thomas More, and posited instead the Abbey of Thelema, full of flowers and wine, heaven and desires, where women and men had come together under the motto "Do as you please."

Providence

Norwich

New Bed

Newport

New London

Montauk

Long Island

Atlantic
Ocean

Atlantic
Ocean

● Plymouth

Bay of Cape Cod

● Barnstable

aushon
sland

Martha's Vineyard

Nantucket Island

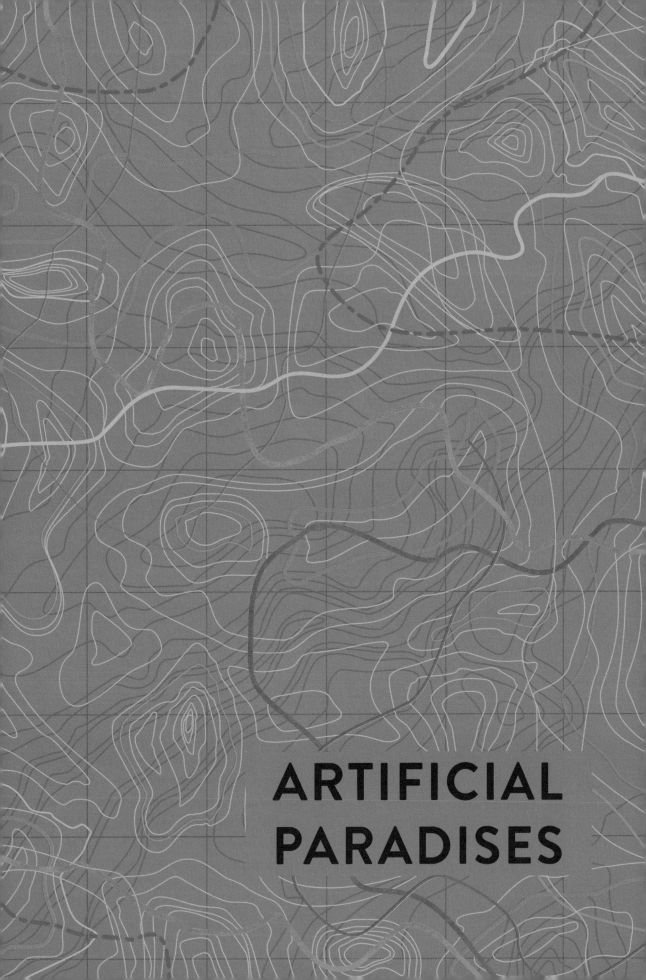

ARTIFICIAL
PARADISES

HOHENSCHWANGAU CASTLE

The Paradise of a Lost Childhood

EUROPE • 47°33' N, 10°74' E

King Ludwig II of Bavaria (1845–1886) spent the first years of his life in Hohenschwangau Castle, near Munich. He called it his "childhood paradise," and nothing would ever console him for having lost his Garden of Eden.

The king hardly governed. He was better at building castles, the most beautiful of which, the vertiginous Neuschwanstein, thrust high into the sky and the night and most suited his solitary disposition, his romantic streak, his angelic figure, and his sadness. When Walt Disney designed the castles of his amusement parks, Neuschwanstein served as their model.

Fascinated by Richard Wagner, whom he offered a theater, King Ludwig II thought himself the keeper of the Holy Grail, just like his beloved Parsifal. Although possibly gay, he was attracted to his cousin Sissi, the wife of Austrian emperor Franz Joseph, yet he would end up marrying Sophie, Sissi's sister. But the marriage didn't work out. Later he would often meet Sissi on Rose Island, in the middle of Lake Starnberg.

Some nights the windows of his castles would be lit up: he would think he was giving an elaborate dinner for Louis XIV, Tristan and Iseult, or a medieval sultan. The king with the beautiful angelic face had become a rather large, puffy gentleman. Declared insane, he would be interned at Berg Castle on June 12, 1886. The next day, he took a stroll along the lake with his psychiatrist, Dr. Bernhard von Gudden. The bodies of the two men would later be found drowned.

Ludwig II had asked for all the castles he had built to be destroyed upon his death, as if to recover, in the beyond, the paradise of his lost childhood.

Ludwig II had asked for all the castles he had built to be destroyed upon his death, as if to recover, in the beyond, the paradise of his lost childhood. Thus lived and died, between castles, lakes, and islands of flowers, King Ludwig II, whom the Bavarians call tenderly the "unhappy king."

96

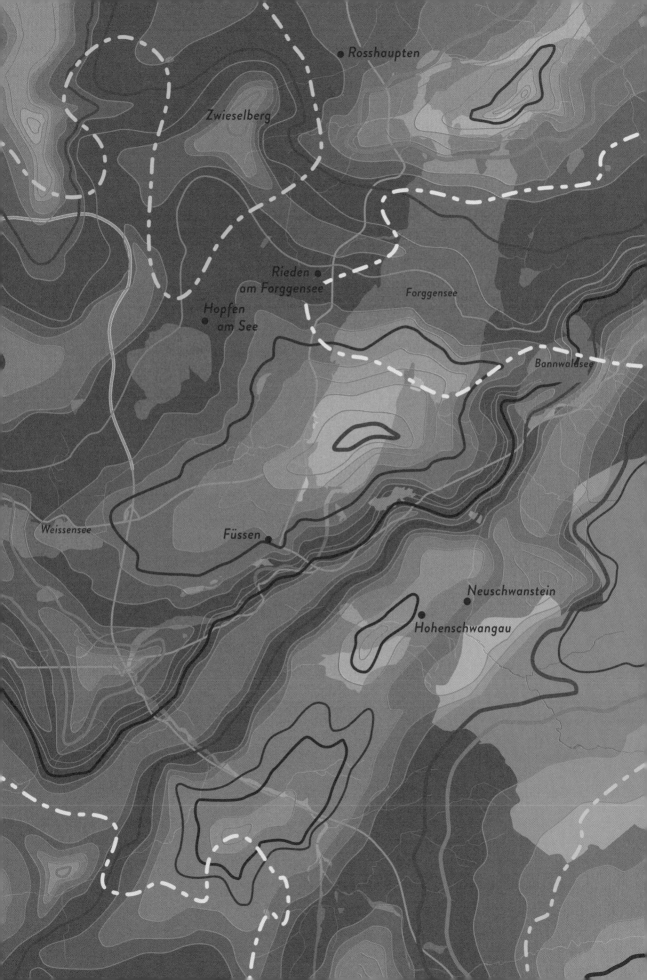

THE COURT OF ELEANOR OF AQUITAINE

The Garden of Courtly Love

EUROPE • 46°34' N, 00°20' E

The most beautiful garden of the Middle Ages did not exist at all. It is nestled among the pages of manuscripts and in the colors of their illuminations. A famous verse epic, the *Roman de la Rose*, presents its fountains and grottoes. Two authors wrote this allegory in two stages, developing the themes of courtly love (or "fin'amor" as the Catalans would say). Guillaume de Lorris began the text in 1220. Fifty years later, Jean de Meun continued the poem. These two bards were so enamored with their subject matter that it took them twenty-two thousand verses to cover it.

A young knight goes for a walk and passes a garden. He is dazzled by it and would like to enter. "Believe me, I thought that I was truly in the earthly paradise. So delightful was the place" (translated by Charles Dahlberg).

But, like all gardens, like all paradises, in fact, this one was locked. It was surrounded by a very high wall. But then, "Idleness" personified opens a door and the poet enters. He discovers a large, square orchard planted with thirty-six species of trees. He sees gentle beasts and perceives flowers, colors, and birds. At the center a fountain was bubbling "under a pine tree." There was a lake, still like a millpond. A thousand verses later, the poet perceives in the reflections of the lake a rose "as live as the most beautiful living creature." This rose is a wom-

an. The narrator would like to pluck it, but it is surrounded by thorns, brambles, and nettles. Vice and misfortune lurk around her, as does "danger," symbolized by her husband's jealousy. "But there were so many thorns, thistles, and brambles that I hadn't the power to pass through the thicket of thorns and reach the rosebud." The knight grows a little discouraged: "I would rather have been dead than alive."

This rose, its beauty, and the thorns that defend her are emblems on the coat of arms of medieval women. Ladies of high standing, associated with Eleanor of Aquitaine, intended to wrest women from the hopelessness of their situation. The Bible, the Church Fathers, and pastors would repeat over and over again that Eve was the reason for the original sin and the Fall from paradise. A slave to her desires, cunning, cruel, and a liar, a woman is "beholden to her womb." Clerics would advise husbands to beat their wives from time to time: "That will teach her." Eleanor and her beautiful girlfriends did not like being beaten. They sounded the alarm bell. Gentle, glowing, and silky soft, the insurrection of women tucked at the heartstrings of society. Marriage was its target. Husbands were vulgar, jealous, and ill behaved. They needed to be reformed. The woman was seen as the whore, the servant, and the injured party.

So she took charge. She would become the dominant party, and man her vassal.

Marriage was not abolished; it was just taken down a notch. Procreation was no longer the supreme goal of love. Adultery was no longer an abomination. Women had the right to take a lover. "Love cannot exert its powers between two people who are married to each other," wrote Andreas Capellanus (translated by John Jay Parry). For lovers give each other everything freely, under no compulsion of necessity, but married people are in duty bound to give in to each other's desires and deny themselves to each other in nothing."

Gentle, glowing, and silky soft, the insurrection of women tucked at the heartstrings of society.

It remained to be seen what the lady would make of this lover. Courtly love did not justify free love, vice, or debauchery. If it loosened the bonds of marriage, it did not replace them with anarchy. Rather, it multiplied the rules, prohibitions, and punishments to the point that courtly love is sometimes described as an invitation to absolute chastity. I think of it more as a way of intensify-

ing desire precisely because of the brambles and thorns that surround the object of desire.

And where is paradise in all this? Did the ladies of Aquitaine reopen its gates? There is nothing to suggest that. Indeed, Eleanor rarely complied with the rules of courtly love. The granddaughter of the troubadour Guillaume d'Aquitaine, who was an expert in courtly love, Eleanor went her own way—and hers was a lively way. At age fifteen she married her first king, Louis VII of France. Enamored with the sound of battles, she pushed her big, powerful king to join the Second Crusade. She succumbed to her desires when she met a very noble man, Lord Raymond of Poitiers—who was also her uncle. She was called a whore and incestuous, which allowed her to get a divorce. She married her second king, the handsome Henri Plantagenet, king of England, who cheated on her and tricked her one day dressed as a page, only to lock her up in a convent. All these trials and tribulations did not prevent her from having eight children, including Richard the Lionheart and John Lackland. At an advanced age and slightly mad, she embarked on a career as a grandmother. She liked her granddaughter Blanche of Castile very much, who would become the mother of King Louis the Saint. Well, it looks like this is what happens when you make too much courtly love.

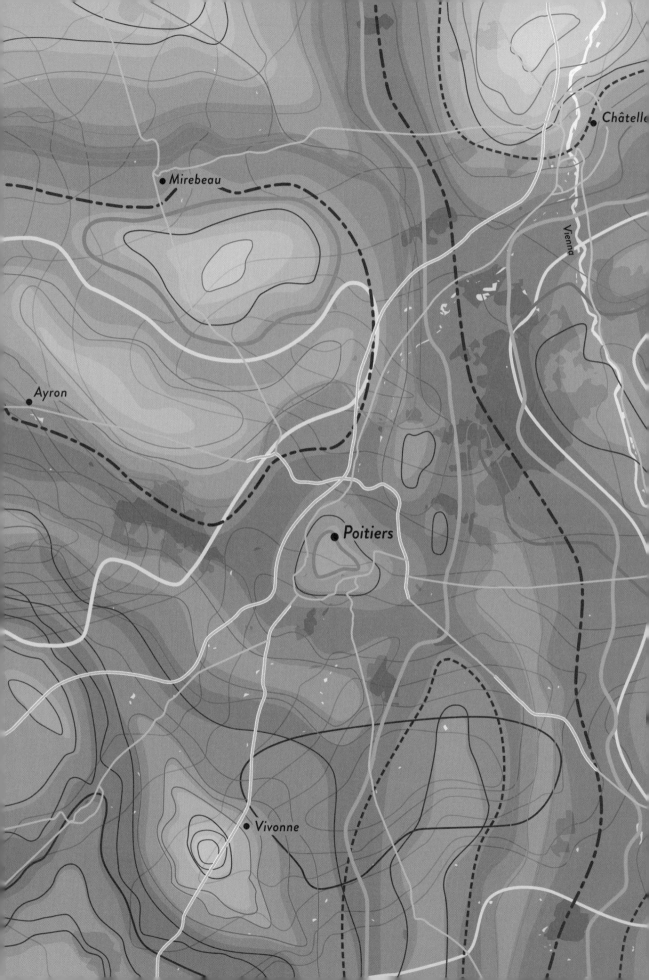

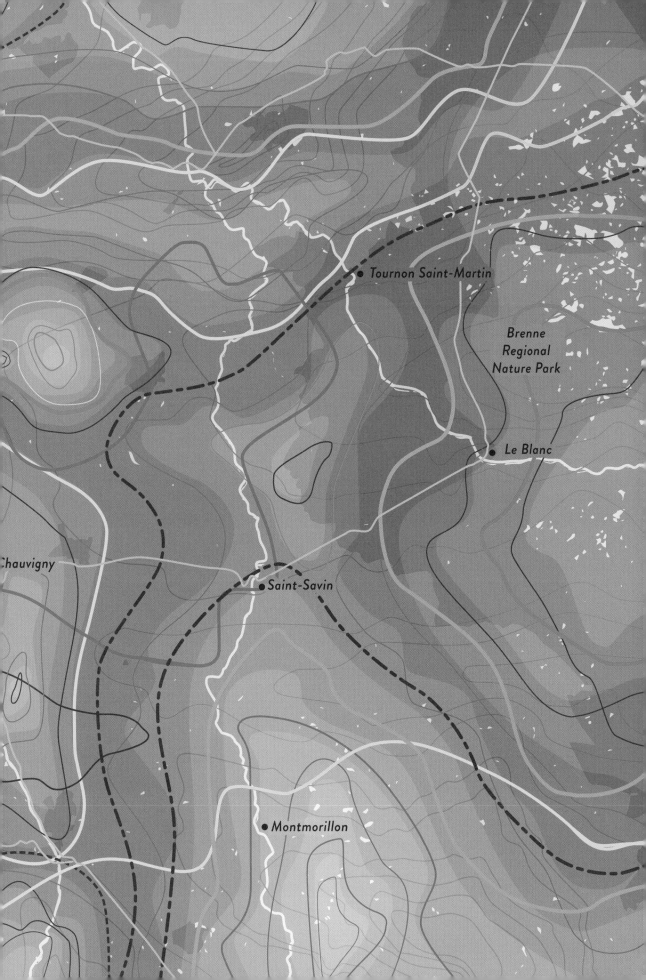

Tournon Saint-Martin

Brenne
Regional
Nature Park

Le Blanc

Chauvigny

Saint-Savin

Montmorillon

THE CITY OF MANOA

Genesis in America

———————

SOUTH AMERICA • 20°05' S, 51°00' W

Gold is excellent; gold is treasure, and he that possesses it does all that he wishes to in this world, and succeeds in helping souls into paradise.

—Christophe Colomb

Christopher Columbus wondered where paradise might be. He looked for it in books and lost hope. "I do not find, nor ever have found, any account by the Romans or Greeks that fixes in a positive manner the site of the terrestrial Paradise." And when he cast off from Palos in 1492, he did not set his course on Eden, or even America—the latter of which did not exist yet. He was headed for Asia, in the footsteps of the very Marco Polo who had struck up a friendship with the Great Khan two centuries earlier.

As a precaution, he had recruited an interpreter for Semitic languages, Luis de Torres, to join the *Santa Maria* crew. Torres had recently converted to Christianity. His name used to be Yosef ben HaLevi Halviri, and he was perhaps a rabbi. He would come in handy one day if they happened upon old Jewish merchants or even, with a little luck, the descendants of the ten lost tribes of Israel.

Columbus was quite mistaken. He got his coordinates for Asia wrong, and if he is said to have found anything, it would be America—which did not yet exist. There were certainly moments when he perceived small corners of paradise. He would be jubilant then. On his third trip he told the Catholic monarchs Ferdinand and Isabella, "I have arrived in another world, in the blessed place where our forefathers lived." A few years later, Amerigo Vespucci, a scholar and geographer, would confirm precisely that. He even provided a description of the inhabitants of Eden: "They are all naked, affable, and of great size."

Soon enough the Spaniards would send thousands of soldiers dressed like crustaceans, with spiky antennas, daggers, and blunderbusses, into the forests, as well as thousands of messengers, lamas, pigs, scriveners, and dogs trained to maul Indigenous people, not to mention a couple of furious and often-hallucinating captains from Extremadura. The Spaniards called paradise El Dorado—the golden one—and all these soldiers hoped to discover sources of gold. In the meantime, they set up a kitty with necklaces and sparkling ornaments, even if that meant ripping them off an Aztec emperor whose head they had cut off.

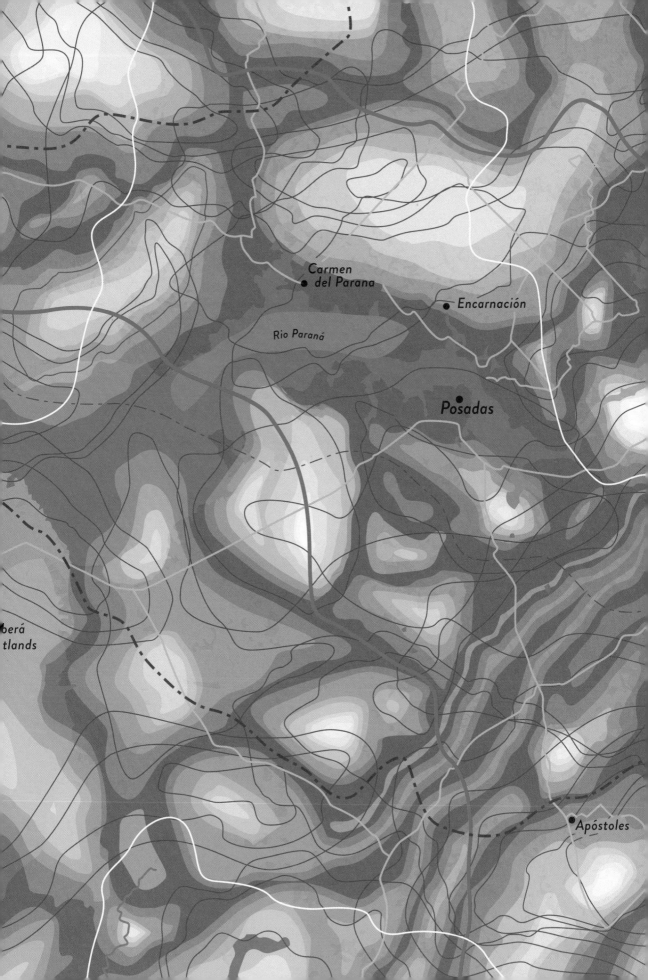

Carmen
del Parana

Encarnación

Rio Paraná

Posadas

berá
tlands

Apóstoles

One day, Private Martinez gets lost in the jungle. He gets mad, runs about, and discovers an El Dorado on the Río Negro, not far from the Paraná River. On the banks of the river is a city made of precious stones: Manoa. Its benevolent ruler receives Martinez and shows him around emerald and golden palaces. Martinez is dazzled but bids the ruler to excuse himself because he must rejoin his troops. The ruler says, "Fair enough," and he arranges an escort for him.

Martinez was not very literate. So we are lucky that he met a chic adventurer, an English-

The Spaniards called paradise El Dorado—the golden one— and all these soldiers hoped to discover sources of gold.

man, one part poet and many parts pirate, Sir Walter Raleigh, who acts as interpreter and describes the city of Manoa for us.

After a century of Spanish wars, a Castilian scholar, Antonio de León Pinelo, drew up a plan for this paradise. His book *El Paraíso en el Nuevo Mundo* has eight hundred pages. He argues that the Bible was wrong and that the rivers of paradise are not at all the Tigris, Euphrates, Ganges, and Indus but the Amazon, the Orinoco, the Río de la Plata, and the Madeleine.

In his fervor, León Pinelo relocated all of Genesis. The origins of humanity are now in America. It was not on Mount Ararat, in western Armenia, that Noah's ark got stranded but in the Andes. León Pinelo lists his evidence: Noah took his three sons, Cham, Shem, and Japheth, with him, as well as his daughter, who is probably the daughter of Enoch whom Cain begot when he lived east of Eden. In addition, he took about fifty cousins and many beasts, including giant ones such as lions, elephants, and hippopotamus. So Noah's ship must have been enormous. And since the forests of the Middle East, even those of Lebanon, are scarce, it is clear that the masts for the Ark must have been carved from the giant sequoias of the western slope of the Andes.

The Portuguese, on the other hand, who discovered Brazil in 1500, were not so interested in paradise. They were realistic, wary, and maybe a little downtrodden and had foresight. They were merchants, not dreamers. They had no interest in the exuberant lyricism of the Spaniards. Epiphanies, trumpets of doom, first-millennium celebrations: all of this was Greek to the subjects of King Manuel, who was known as the "sad king." You wouldn't find locos of the likes of Lope de Aguirre or Hernando Pizarro among them. For them, every penny counted, and if by accident they had bagged a paradise, they certainly would not brag about it; instead they would have resold it or put it in reserve for a rainy day. While waiting for that day, they preferred to grow cotton, enslave Indigenous and Black people, and destroy the splendid forests of brazilwood to sell to Europe.

In the seventeenth century a Portuguese Jesuit by the name of Simão de Vasconcelos admitted that Brazil boasted some gardens of delights, but he is tongue-bound on the detail. He dedicated barely seven paragraphs to these paradises on the other side of the world. A century later, another Jesuit, Sebastião da Rocha Pita, confirmed his observation. He took the opportunity to relocate all of sacred history to the American continent because Brazil boasted a fruit called *maracujá*, a "mysterious gift of nature that, with the same elements with which it composed a flower, forged the instruments of the Holy Passion." The beautiful flower of the passion fruit is in the shape of a cross and reproduces in its cup the five wounds of Christ, thus commemorating the tragedy on the Mount of Olives.

The discretion of the Portuguese is astonishing. Why did they claim to never have seen these paradises that dazzled their Spanish neighbors and rivals? They must have been aware that, so far, most paradises had ended badly. Maybe they did not want to experience a few moments of joy to then inadvertently commit a sin and find themselves to the east of Eden until the end of eternity.

On the banks of the river is a city made of precious stones: Manoa.

HOLMBY HILLS

Walt Disney, a Pacified Miniature Universe

Walt Disney is famous. He made masterpieces, invented Mickey Mouse and Bambi, and created visual impressions of Alice in Wonderland, Pinocchio, and Snow White and the Seven Dwarves. In 1949 he suddenly felt the urge to build a miniature railroad in his large garden in Holmby Hills, Los Angeles: the Carolwood Pacific Railroad, whose steam engine he dubbed Lilly Belle, after his wife. He created artificial hills for the pretty Western Railroad locomotive to snake through, trailing smoke.

He created a children's universe, parallel to the real world, that was peaceful and without sin, eternally renewed itself, was purged from the ravages of time, and was separated from reality by "mysterious barricades."

As small trains go, this one is quite large: passengers are able to sit in the carriages with their legs tucked under. But it remains modest in size compared to its role model, the Central Pacific Railroad, which it reproduced on a scale of one to eight. Disney drove the train himself. And was very content doing so. A few years later, he would create Disneyland, the first of his parks, each of which would feature one or multiple miniature railroads.

His passion for trains started at a young age. In 1917, during his summer vacations, dressed in a shining uniform, he sold newspapers and candy on the Missouri Pacific Railroad. Thus a passion was formed that explains his taste for small trains and his love of models and tiny decorations, and also why he would use drawings to create a children's universe, parallel to the real world, that was peaceful and without sin, eternally renewed itself, was purged from the ravages of time, and was separated from reality by "mysterious barricades." "I want Disneyland to be the most wonderful place on Earth, and I want a train to run through it." This is the North American version of paradise.

Walt Disney is not doing anything new. He follows in a tradition that strives for humanity to experiment with softened, smoothed, and disinfected versions of reality. Faced

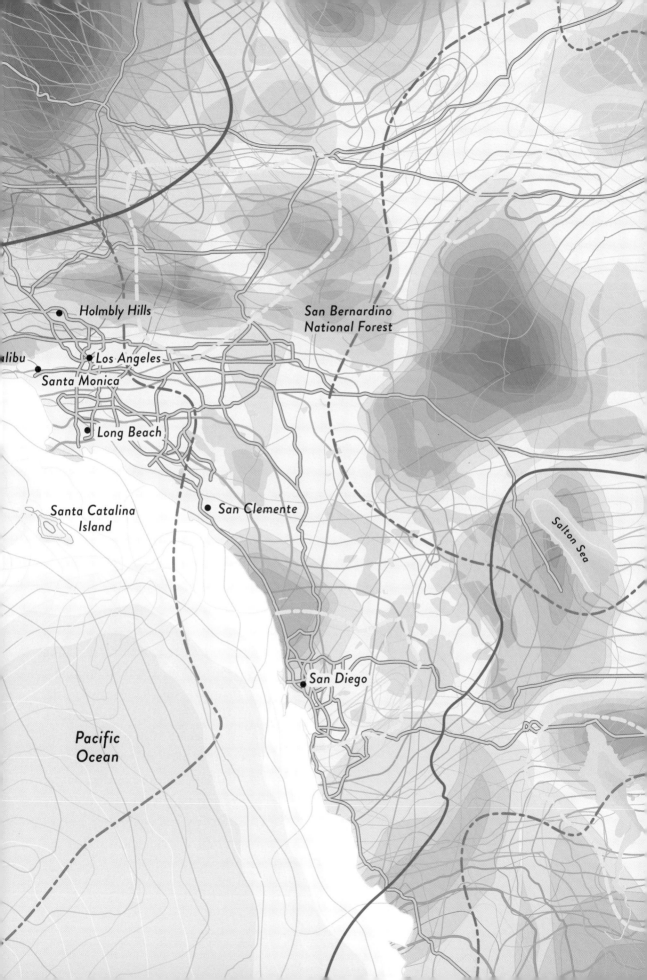

Holmbly Hills

San Bernardino
National Forest

Malibu

Los Angeles

Santa Monica

Long Beach

Santa Catalina
Island

San Clemente

Salton Sea

San Diego

Pacific
Ocean

with the enormity and chaos of the Creation, humans feel weak and aimless.

Even the emperor of China is tiny compared to the mountains, the clouds, the sea, and the true masters of things: gods, dragons, and demons. Miniature worlds are pacified universes whose double charm is that they let one ignore the "evil" that the gods have giddily inflicted upon the earth, and to be tiny, which allows humanity to perceive it as a whole, to look at it from above, to direct and fix it. Miniatures are "metaphysical coup d'états." They are on the tricky mission of "encompassing infinity." Thanks to them, humans become larger than the universe. The child who pushes their locomotive on rails without accident or unwanted surprises is taking a break from the world whose hostage and plaything they are. The child assumes the place of kings and gods and reigns. The kid resides in paradise.

Each morning, Chinese emperor Hsien Tung (thirteenth century) took his bath and had a map of his vast empire brought to him by his majordomos. He would follow the bends of the Yangtze River, the mountains of the Liaodong Peninsula, and the glaciers of Tibet with his fingertips. He would contemplate the territory he commanded. He would look at the deserts or cities he had never even visited. He would regard the entirety of his prerogative as if through a mouse hole. And he could put in order this mess that the gods had left behind.

"I want Disneyland to be the most wonderful place on Earth, and I want a train to run through it."

Marcel Proust was like Emperor Hsien Tung but more "expeditious": to forge himself a universe that was simultaneously docile, calm, small, and orderly, he had only to read "the Almanach de Gotha and the railroad directory."

Emperor Hadrian had a lake dug out in the villa he built in Tivoli to resemble the Mediterranean Sea, and eighteenth-century Swedish naturalist Carl Linnaeus shrank the vastness of the earth with all its chaos by incarcerating all living beings in a dictionary that subjected the jumble of plants and animals to a perfect logic, using barely three words to describe each species.

Not all miniatures are benevolent. If most of them seek to re-create paradise and mainly play a role in childhood and recall memories thereof, some others operate in the service of evil. All the oldies out there who once played with tin soldiers will remember the battles that these figures fought.

Certainly, as with miniature trains, the child who plays with tin soldiers occupies a dominant position, that of the giant or the master. The child is larger than the universe they hold in their hands. The kid is the big gun here. But if, as is the case with mini trains, the child has power over a well-oiled, ordered universe where derailments can quickly be repaired, the young person playing with tin soldiers is surrounded by chaos, wickedness, suffering, and death. It is in the bilge water of horror that the painted soldiers operate. Hussars, zouaves, and musketeers defending no nation at all will be sentenced by the child as "destined for death." Their innards spill out; they lose an eye or a leg.

The child who pushes their locomotive on rails without accident or unwanted surprises is taking a break from the world whose hostage and plaything they are. The child assumes the place of kings and gods and reigns. The kid resides in paradise.

If Walt Disney's little train blows a string of smoke into the calm sky and the suburbs of paradise, the wars of tin soldiers play out in hell. The child who commands them hardly resembles the god of mercy. They are wearing Beelzebub's uniform; they are the Lord of the Flies. The gates of heaven are closed again. The tin soldiers are cursed and far removed from bliss. Their maneuvers take place east of Eden.

109

THE MAUSOLEUM OF QIN SHI HUANG

Deceiving Death to Gain Paradise

———◆———

Chinese emperor Qin Shi Huang did not want to die. There might be a paradise after death, but the one promised by Buddha, Laozi, or Confucius is a rather vague concept, so much so that Qin Shi Huang (or Shi Huangdi) took matters into his own hands. As a first step he tried to trick death. If, in spite of his tricks, death would find him in the end, he arranged to spend eternity in a small paradise of his own making, a space where death's closest ally, time—a power that mutilates and kills—would be kept at bay. This kingdom of darkness and stagnation may not be worthy of a true Eden, but it was better than nothing—better than nothingness.

The life of the emperor was a game of hide-and-seek with death. No one knew where Qin Shi Huang lived. He seemed not to exist. His residence had 270 palaces, and his servants spent their days wondering in which room he was sleeping. Despite his precautions, and since he was so suspicious, he still feared that one of his butlers would spot him and tell death where he was. So he had an ace up his sleeve: he disguised himself as one of his own butlers so as to confuse death. Should death still try to strike, it would target one of his servants instead and make him pass away in his place.

This kingdom of darkness and stagnation may not be worthy of a true Eden, but it was better than nothing—better than nothingness.

Qin Shi Huang forbade his servants to ever tell him if he was sick. His fevers were a state secret that was even kept from Qin Shi Huang himself. If a servant defied this rule, they would be liquidated. In addition, if the worst did happen, it would be sacrilegious to announce his death. Thus, if the end did arrive, Qin Shi Huang would not be told, and thus death would be caught out.

One day he nevertheless died.

And everyone held their tongues lest Qin Shi Huang should find out about it. His body was placed in a car that would bring

him to his last resting place in Lintong County, Shaanxi Province. On his journey he was served meals so as not to grow suspicious. The convoy arrived at the tomb. It had been carefully, and secretly, prepared, although seven hundred thousand workers had worked on it for more than thirty years. When the funeral ceremony was over, the workers, who were putting the final touches to the mausoleum, were locked into the tomb and died trapped inside.

The tomb remains unopened to this day, not because the Communist authorities complied with Qin Shi Huang's wishes, but because the vault is mined with crossbows that would shoot arrows at the first intruder. Moreover, archeologists prefer to wait until science has advanced enough to allow them to enter the tomb without damaging it (not far from there, about 1 mile [1.6 kilometers] away, the same emperor had famously buried eight thousand terra-cotta statues representing his army).

We have a description of the tomb because historian Sima Qian (145–86 BCE) was able to enter it. Workers had reconstituted a kingdom underground that re-created

exactly the one over which Qin Shi Huang ruled. Albeit of a different scale: instead of an almost infinite territory, the tomb is a shrunken version, but faithful to its model. It escapes time, all the vexations that time inflicts on things and beings, and keeps withering and agony at bay.

The tomb reproduces the size of China but in miniature, following the approach of many paradises; for example, Walt Disney's small trains. China is recognizable in it, with its mountains and its hundred rivers sloshing with mercury, which have been left unharmed by time. The emperor had made his choice: he preferred geography, which is immovable, to history, which changes all the time.

This empire in limbo is illuminated by torches lit with seal oil, intended to burn for a very long time. As for plants, they are made of jade, which does not fade and would therefore survive the dirty tricks of aging and death unscathed.

Qin Shi Huang had taken further, more-ambitious measures still to expel time from his territory. His prime minister Li Si was also a man of permanence.

112

He followed the cult of order, logic, classification, and uniformity. He unified weights, currencies, and the scripts in use in the immense empire. And he imposed the same width requirements on the axles of all carts. He loathed anarchy, the unpredictable, and anomalies. He wanted to spare the immense geography from the troubles of history.

Li Si isolated paradise by imprisoning it within a gigantic wall that would stop all kinds of miasmas that could infect the geographies of paradise with the devious topographies that reigned beyond the wall.

And he had a miracle cure against change. It is well known that writers are artful dodgers and that they, under the guise of celebrating the past, actually achieve the opposite: they clear the paths along which the future will travel, this abominable future that Li Si sought to keep at bay. Are books, especially history books, not just the products, witnesses, and manufacturers of time?

"Your Majesty," Li Si proclaimed, "rules over a unified empire. It has separated black from white. . . . Yet, independent schools are teaming up to critique the codes of laws and regulations. . . . Your Servant suggests that all books in the imperial archives, except the memoirs of Ts'in, be burned."

We will get a better measure of the emperor and his prime minister's ambitions if we recall that it was under the reign of Qin Shi Huang that the construction of the Great Wall of China was completed. It makes perfect sense: Li Si knew well that all paradises eventually implode. That is why the person who put Qin Shi Huang in power took plenty of precautions himself: Li Si banished time by destroying all books. And he isolated paradise by imprisoning it within a gigantic wall that would stop all kinds of miasmas that could infect the geographies of paradise with the devious topographies that reigned beyond the wall.

THE LAND OF NOD

On the Threshold of Paradise

ASIA • 34°31' N, 69°07' E

And I saw a new heaven and a new earth: for the first heaven and the first earth were passed away.

—Revelation

In the Middle Ages it was not uncommon for a man to mount an expedition to find paradise. When he had spotted one, he would push the gate open and sneak into the beautiful garden—but this sort of thing did not happen very often. In fact, this kind of undertaking was almost hopeless because the Bible did not offer many clues or directions. We just about know that a spring flowed in the center of Eden that created four rivers. The first was the river Pishon, or Pison, which encircled the land of Havilah, rich in gold, resin, and carnelian. The second river was the Gihon, which irrigated the land of Kush. The other two are more familiar to us now, the rivers Tigris and Euphrates.

Geographers located the Garden of Eden on their world maps on the basis of these details. The Tigris and Euphrates flow in the country we call Iraq today, which borders Israel. Kush probably refers to present-day Ethiopia. The Gihon River would therefore be the Red Sea. The Pishon has never been located by anyone, but research found recently that a river of this name once flowed into the Arabian Gulf, though there is no trace of it today. In conclusion: the Garden of Eden occupied roughly the location of Palestine, which is hardly surprising, since the prophecies of Ezekiel and Isaiah predicted as much. We may even assume that the Lord, by driving Adam and Eve out of Palestine, had announced the long exodus a part of the people of Israel would have to endure for two millennia.

This enigma had barely been solved before another, even more puzzling one arose. What happened to the inhabitants of Eden when it closed its doors? The cursed couple got on all right. Yes, it was deprived of paradise, but there is a life after paradise. Adam and Eve went about their business and loved each other. When she was 120, Eve gave birth to another child, a boy named Seth. Other children followed.

That's all we know about our forebears. But what about their offspring? Adam and Eve had two sons: Cain, the elder, and Abel. Abel was pretty gentle. Cain killed him and the Lord was disgruntled.

He sent Cain to a dreadful land, the Land of Nod, which was made of stones, grass, and shrubs. Cain would have thirty-three sons and twenty-four daughters, recounts Jewish historian Flavius Josephus.

One might think that this Land of Nod was a kind of hell, or at least a rough draft—a first model of hell. But the Lord does not help us much in our investigation because he is very secretive and confuses the issue.

One might think that this Land of Nod was a kind of hell, or at least a rough draft, a first model of hell.

When Cain, interrogated by God, admits to having killed his brother, the Lord is surprised. And he is furious. "What hast thou done? the voice of thy brother's blood crieth unto me from the ground. And now art thou cursed from the earth, which hath opened her mouth to receive thy brother's blood from thy hand." He is sentenced: Cain is to be exiled to the Land of Nod. This country extends east of Eden so should be next to Afghanistan, where the sun rises, but modern researchers have a different idea: Nod as a land lies nowhere; it is a land that is forever vague, without beginning or end, without borders, and whose occupants are destined to walk the earth for eternity without the possibility of absolution. Those who are cursed would be without a home or hearth, vagabonds, wanderers.

When the verdict falls, Cain begs the Lord: "Behold, thou hast driven me out this day from the face of the earth, and from thy face shall I be hid, and I shall be a fugitive and a vagabond in the earth, and it shall come to pass that every one that findeth me shall slay me."

Cain's fear is surprising. We know from Genesis that at that time, the earth was populated by only three people: the original couple, Adam and Eve, and their descendants, of which there was only one left, Cain, since he had killed his brother Abel. Under these circumstances it is hard to see where these bandits could come from that worry Cain. Yet, the Lord is not surprised. He even goes so far as to reassure Cain: "Therefore whosoever slayeth Cain," he replies, "vengeance shall be taken on him sevenfold." And as a precaution, he places a mark on Cain "lest any finding him should kill him."

Is God showing his clemency? Or perhaps his ferociousness. God seems to have understood that the cruelest punishment would be to deprive a man of his death.

"Guilty," rules the judge. "I condemn you

Nod as a land lies nowhere;

it is a land that is forever vague,

without beginning or end.

not to die!" Cain is imprisoned for eternity in the endless land, the Land of Nod, without cardinal points or borders.

God is not done surprising us. With him we jump from one shock to the next. Genesis tells us that Cain, now that he is in his vast open-air prison, his infinite prison, "knew his wife; and she conceived and bore Enoch." A woman? But what was she doing in a land like this? Did she commit a felony, too, and was serving a sentence? And who were her parents? She could only be the daughter of Adam and Eve, even though the Bible never told us that the original couple had, besides two boys, a daughter.

Or did this woman, like the bandits who frightened Cain so much, belong to another human lineage? But the Bible excludes such a hypothesis. It does not budge on its stipulation: Adam and Eve are the parents of all of humankind, and there is no other lineage; one point of origin, that's it. The Scripture confirms this: God "hath made of one blood all nations of men for to dwell on all the face of the earth" (Acts 17:26).

So? So we must give up our guessing game. And what's even more disconcerting: we must assume that this woman is the daughter of Eve and Adam. But in that case, she would be Cain's sister. And if she made love to him, she committed—they committed together—the sin of incest.

These are the beginnings of our journey: Adam and Eve eat the forbidden fruit. One of their sons murders his brother, after which he sleeps with his sister and makes her children—what a nice list of achievements! This family is in the hands of God, but they go their own way. They dislike beaten tracks. They provoke, murder, disobey, practice incest, enjoy themselves, blaspheme, and overturn the laws. Rebellion, sin, and evil deeds are our oldest companions. We love freedom more than happiness, it seems.

117

THE CLOCK

A Model of Paradise

———

Sometimes people get tired of the disorderly societies designed by history. They then busy themselves with establishing and constructing the ideal city, egalitarian and perfect, without suffering or ugly sores—smooth, monotonous, and untouched by time. From their magic cauldrons arise calm cities, free from evil and inhabited by peaceful people, and they call them paradises. The mechanical clock, which was invented in the late Middle Ages, was one of these artificial cities, and at least the model for one of these paradises.

Exactly how the clock came about is a secret. No one knows the name of the man who succeeded, by a silent stroke of genius, to catch the wild time, put it in his retorts, and replace it with a time that chimes to another beat, an equalized time, without wear or tear, a time saved from time. The greatest scientific discovery of history was invented by a "nobody." Yet, we know where this discovery was made. The first mechanical clocks were probably made by a German monk between the eleventh and thirteenth centuries. It makes sense: the late Middle Ages were in upheaval, torn apart by wars, a move away from the Second Coming, extreme poverty, the fear of the Apocalypse and the unexpected. In this context the monastery and the mechanical clock constituted the only two structures to provide a form of order with which humanity was able to counteract nothingness and chaos.

Convents work like clockwork anyway. The regularity of prayers, getting up, mealtimes, work and bedtime, irrespective of the seasons, splits time with the same rigor as clocks do with their weights and escapements. Subjected to life without hiccups or surprises, the communities that make up a monastery are perfect: isolated, dismissive of the agonies of history, unaffected by the frenzy of psychology, they form little paradises. Monks have left their identity, their desires, and their passions at the gates of the monastery. They gave their celibacy vows, which freed them from the chain of generations, from memory and hope. They fled the labyrinths of time. Every day is simultaneously yesterday and tomorrow.

Open a watchcase and observe the steady, impassive, and fatal movement of the works, the mainspring and hammer mechanism, the fourth wheel, and the hands, and you will perceive a miniature paradise.

As in Eden, there is no mystery and no wear and tear, no diseases, no influenza, and no accidents. Time, the father of sorrow and disease, the father of death; time itself is dead. No more suffering and no more injustice.

No more death. Paradise belongs to us—but what a strange paradise it is!

Dostoevsky, who was an orthodox Christian, did not like these paradises removed from human tragedy. He wondered why God, when sorting out his affairs, had refused to make the world as perfect a mechanism as a watchcase. He proposed an explanation in *Notes from the Underground*, by using the metaphor not of the movement of a watch but that of piano keys. He writes: "Then, you say, science itself will teach man . . . that he never has really had any caprice or will of his own, and that he himself is something of the nature of a piano key or the stop of an organ. . . . All human actions will then, of course, be tabulated according to these laws, mathematically, like tables of logarithms . . . ; there would be published certain edifying works of the nature of encyclopaedic lexicons, in which everything will be so clearly calculated and explained that there will be no more incidents or adventures in the world. . . . Then the 'Palace of Crystal' will be built. Then . . . in fact, those will be halcyon days" (translated by Constance Garnett).

Happiness, and an automatized paradise then. But Dostoevsky, the man of the underground, hated these "palaces of crystal." The man from the underground screams: "And why are you so firmly, so triumphantly, convinced that only the normal and the positive —in other words, only what is conducive to welfare —is for the advantage of man? . . . Perhaps he is just as fond of suffering? Perhaps suffering is just as great a benefit to him as well-being? Man is sometimes extraordinarily, passionately, in love with suffering, and that is a fact. . . . And yet, I think man will never renounce real suffering; that is, destruction and chaos."

Dostoevsky made his choice: freedom over automatized happiness. He writes about humans: "He would even risk his cakes and would deliberately desire the most fatal rubbish, the most uneconomical absurdity, simply to introduce into all this positive good sense his fatal fantastic element. It is just his fantastic dreams, his vulgar folly that he will desire to retain, simply in order to prove to himself —as though that were so necessary —that men still are men and not the keys of a piano. . . . And that is not all: even if man really were nothing but a piano key, even if this were proved to him by natural science and mathematics, even then he would not become reasonable but would purposely do something perverse out of simple ingratitude, simply to gain his point. And if he does not find means, he will contrive destruction and chaos, will contrive sufferings of all sorts, only to gain his point!"

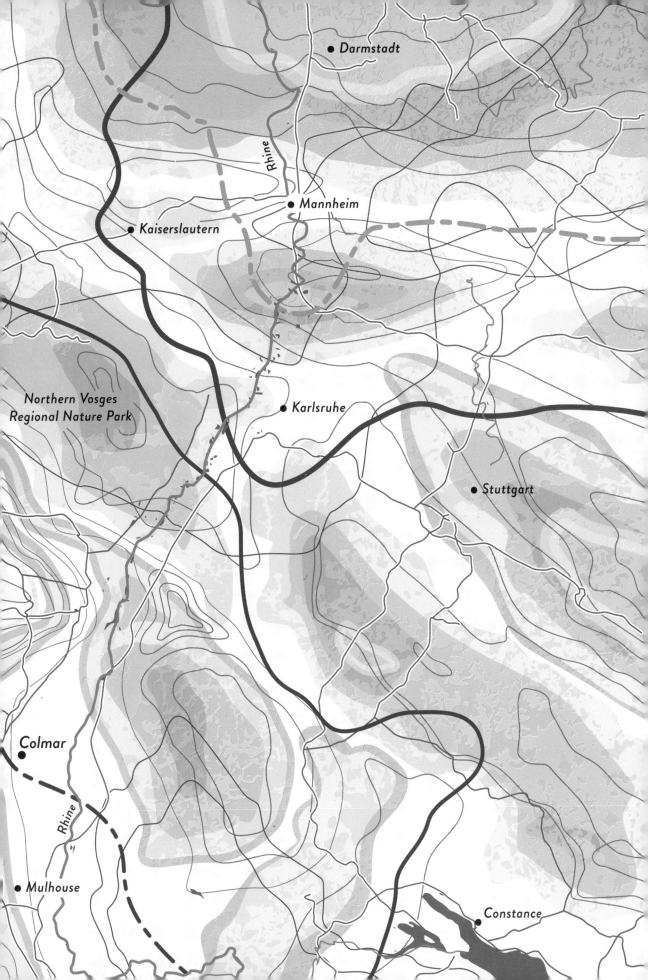

IN THE SAME COLLECTION: